Multiply Your Business Value Through Brand & AI

Multiply Your Business Value Through Brand & AI

Rajan Narayan

BEP

BUSINESS EXPERT PRESS

Leader in applied, concise business books

Multiply Your Business Value Through Brand & AI

Copyright © Business Expert Press, LLC, 2022.

Cover design by Charlene Kronstedt

Interior design by Exeter Premedia Services Private Ltd., Chennai, India

First published in 2021 by
Business Expert Press, LLC
222 East 46th Street, New York, NY 10017
www.businessexpertpress.com

ISBN-13: 978-1-63742-107-9 (paperback)
ISBN-13: 978-1-63742-108-6 (e-book)

Business Expert Press Marketing Collection

Collection ISSN: 2169-3978 (print)
Collection ISSN: 2169-3986 (electronic)

First edition: 2021

10 9 8 7 6 5 4 3 2 1

For Geeta. Always the inspiration for the good things
I've done in my life.

Description

Building brands and creating brand value is believed to be long term, esoteric, hard to put a value to and mostly, driven by creativity. The field has lost ground in this current age of venture capital valuations, where customer acquisition and gross value added (GVA) have been given priority by valuators. Unfortunately, this is detrimental to an organization, as brand building can multiply the valuation of an enterprise. Artificial intelligence (AI), on the other hand, is a replacement for doing mundane repetitive tasks in organizations. AI and machine learning help organizations reduce errors, build efficiencies and increase profitability, thereby freeing the human capital to perform more intellectual tasks. This book presents the case for using AI to help organizations build brands effectively and optimally, thereby enhancing the overall value of the organization.

This book is ideal for entrepreneurs, investors, CEOs, brand and marketing heads of organizations, as it will provide them pathways and routes of using AI to build strong customer relationships, thus creating immense brand value. It could also be used as a textbook in courses on Brand Management and as a supplemental text in Marketing Management courses. It is especially relevant in the current environment where many enterprises are being created and funded by professionals who lack a marketing background. On the other hand, marketing, communication and advertising professionals are circumspect of technology and often see it as a "back-office" operation. People often tend to club technology and brand in different buckets and cannot see the correlation between the two. This book breaks such misconceptions and offers a practical approach to brand building using AI that anyone can understand and implement.

Keywords

AI; ML; brand; marketing; advertising; digital; customer; customer-service; brand strategy; communication; brand experience; customer loyalty; customer experience; technology

Contents

Preface

This book is targeted at entrepreneurs, students in business school and professional courses and professional managers. Its objective is to guide them on how they can combine the power of Artificial intelligence (AI) and brand building and generate huge value.

It's based on my experience and learning of over 25 years.

The book is written for businessmen looking to create brand value and who are courageous and willing to try new vistas in pursuit of the same. This book should act as a practical handbook for entrepreneurs, helping them create value through brand and AI.

Acknowledgments

I'm extremely grateful to the following people who took out time from their busy schedules to help give shape to this book.

Dr. Naresh K Malhotra

Govind Pandey

Dr. Milind Agarwal

Raka Sinha

Sundar Narayanan

Renuka Bharadwaj

Udbhav Narayan

A special mention of gratitude to my parents for inculcating in me the thirst for knowledge and the willingness to share it.

CHAPTER 1

Overview

- Key concepts of brand management.
- Defining a brand and examining the different kinds of brands.
- Understanding how consumers interact and decode brands.
- The importance of branding in business.
- Why the principles of branding apply to all kinds of businesses, including business-to-business marketing.
- How building strong brands is beneficial to companies.
- How brand value increases company valuation.
- Examples of companies that have benefited from creating brands.
- Developing brand strategy: Framework and process.
- Introduction to AI, popular misconceptions and the reasons for the rise of AI in recent times.
- Applications areas of AI.
- Advantages of AI.
- How AI benefits us.
- Why AI is here to stay.

Current Situation

It is a well-known fact that in the hospitality industry most hotel properties are owned and managed by franchisees. In fact, the figure as stated in a 2019 report, is as high as 82 percent. In this arrangement, the franchisees invest in the property, hire, train and manage the staff, and run the hotel 365 days of the year. What then is the role of the major hospitality brands? They provide training, set quality standards and conduct regular audits to ensure that the customer is happy and satisfied with the experience. In short, they own nothing but the brand. This allows them to be light on assets, have a steady revenue stream and expand rapidly, making them favorites of stock bourses across the world. So, when Prince Al Waleed Bin Talal of Saudi Arabia and Bill Gates bought Four Seasons Hotels Inc. for $3.8 billion, it could be argued that in essence, they paid that amount purely for the brand.

Thus, brands unlock tremendous value for organizations and businesses. This truth cuts across all kinds of business types, be it fast-moving consumer goods, consumer durables, business-to-business (B2B) companies, technology companies, start-ups, service organizations, consulting firms, health care companies, law firms, not-for-profit organizations, NGOs, universities, and schools, among others. In fact, anything that offers a solution or a service, including people and places can be considered to be a brand. Actors, politicians, political parties, designers, corporate honchos, cities, destinations, monuments and even countries are brands.

So, what is the definition of a brand? And what qualifies a product, service, or solution as a brand?

A brand is anything that you consume willingly because it addresses a particular need that you have, in a manner most suitable to you. This need could be functional, for example, you could be simply wanting to have a bathroom that is clean and odorless or to travel quickly to another city. Or it could be an emotional need such as feeling special at having accomplished a milestone, or looking desirable and fashionable among your friends and peer group.

More often than not, you end up selecting a particular brand for the combination of functional and emotional benefits that it provides. Let's take the bathroom cleaner example. Now while there are many products that can help you clean your bathroom, your selection would depend on the parameters that you believe are important. For example, you may want the product not just for its efficacy but also require that it is gentle on the skin, leaves behind an aromatic fragrance, and also comprises chemicals that aren't harmful to the environment. So, while you began your journey with perhaps a scouring powder in mind, you may end up buying a particular cleaning liquid or gel because it appealed to both, your mind as well as your heart. Moreover, you wouldn't mind paying more for this product because you value the combination of its benefits.

This logic applies to everything that we consume. All of it, including products, services, countries, politicians, rock stars, and movies are brands appealing to our minds and hearts. Take India for example. To your mind it may stand for many things: fast-growing large economy, world's largest democracy, second highest population and perhaps, seventh largest land mass. But your heart may influence you to add to these statistics, images of the Taj Mahal, curries, yoga, mysticism, as well as some famous people of Indian origin. This combined perception of India will decide whether you choose to invest in an Indian start-up or visit India as a tourist in the near future or try out Indian cuisine. This same reasoning is what drives you to pick a particular cola, software, mobile phone, TV, vote for a politician, and it's also the reason why you like a particular actor, singer and cuisine too.

Which is why, everything is a brand, offering its particular blend of rational and emotional benefits that appeals to different types of individuals, carving a market for itself based on that unique blend of benefits. A popular misconception is that branding does not apply in the B2B arena. In B2B selling, every decision is purely rational and sales too happens based on a set of carefully evaluated performance parameters. While this may sound logical, nothing could be further from the truth. Even in B2B selling, emotions play a huge role. Often purchase decisions are taken favoring a particular vendor because the decision makers of the organization felt they "gelled" better with the team from that particular vendor over others. Or because, the selected organization, "shared a common vision" or "shared similar values" with the customer. These are merely terminologies that are used often in B2B selling to rationalize decision making.

Successful brands are those who understand their customer's needs well and tailor their set of rational and emotional benefits to appeal to their customer's needs. Over time, these brands become the first choice for customers and, eventually, a stage is reached when they become the default choice for customers who are loathe to change from the comfort of the brand to another. This provides brands with a unique power called *brand equity* that brands exercise to dominate marketing and selling channels. On the basis of consumer demand, brands negotiate better deals with distribution channels, associates, manufacturers, trade partners and intermediaries to their advantage. Over a period of time, this equity leads to huge savings in cost, increase in profits and guarantees dominant market leadership. This power or equity is what makes a brand an attractive proposition for competitors, potential investors and financial institutions. For a competitor, buying out a powerful rival brand will increase its reach among customers, negotiating power with trade and reduce competitive pressures. For another company that may not be in direct competition with this brand, the purchase of the brand will provide it with access to an entire distribution channel, which it currently may not have access to. For an investor or a private equity firm, brand equity translates into a strong topline and bottom-line performance of the company, making it a worthy stock to include in their portfolio.

Thus, successful brands return huge amounts to their owners on the company balance sheet. This is called *brand value*. There are many methods for calculating brand value, but the real worth of a brand is visible when organizations and brands change hands. When a few years ago, Merck, the German health and pharmaceutical giant, sold its consumer health division to Proctor & Gamble (P&G) for over $4 billion, financial reports opined that when equated with transactions for the sector, the price paid, at approximately 5 times revenue and 20 times profit, seemed on the higher side. But if one were to look at this from the perspective of P&G, this price seemed well worth it, because it provided P&G access to the ready customer base, distribution channel and leverage that the division's brand portfolio enjoyed.

Traditionally, brand creation has been viewed as a long-term activity, involving deep investments to create awareness and maintain brand recall in expensive mediums such as television, newspapers, magazines, radio and outdoor through a structured process called *brand building*. Such deep investments required companies to have dedicated marketing teams that are further specialized in the field of product or brand management, besides augmenting marketing with functional experts and partners to handle various components of marketing such as, research, media planning and buying, advertising management, digital advertising and specialists for packaging, events, activations, public relations and celebrity management. As brands become larger and the process gets more and more complicated, more areas and fields get added and the discipline gets splintered even further to include specialist functions, experts and consultants.

Despite such heavy investments and willingness to give the process time, brand-building activities do not guarantee results. In fact, a summary of various reports tells us that each year more than 30,000 new consumer products are launched and 80 percent of them fail. A lot of these failures are from the stables of some of the best consumer marketing companies in the world. Reports analyzing brand launches list numerous reasons for their failures, from poor selection of the target audience, weak product proposition, unclear messaging and uncoordinated marketing efforts. Therefore, merely pouring huge amounts of money into marketing activities and building specialized teams is no assurance for creating brand value. At the same time, in the same period there have been numerous brands that not just have outpaced their competition but also created entire categories when none existed at a fraction of the cost that traditional marketing companies invest in their brand-building efforts.

What is the difference between these two sets of brands? Both the sets operated in the same environment, both had extremely talented teams working on them and both sets worked in categories that had similar opportunities and barriers. Yet one set failed despite all the backing and support a brand could have, while the other set succeeded even when the odds were stacked against them.

The difference between the two sets is a well-defined and well-executed brand strategy. A well-defined brand strategy clearly articulates the critical factors that determine the success of a brand. This would include outlining the following:

The Brand's Growth Source: This identifies the opportunities for the brand's growth by recognizing competitive categories and brands that could stand to lose business and market share to the brand. It compels the team to relook at the competitive framework through a fresh lens and reorganize prevalent thinking in a new light.

The Brand's Target Audience: This step attempts to go beyond the typical definition of a target audience. It seeks to differentiate between the general and the specific. It identifies the personality differences between people who choose the brand versus those who don't. It recognizes the finer nuances that will help the brand distinguish between its potential customers and other customers with similar profiles.

The Consumer Insight: This step encourages the team to dig deeper and understand the reason for the customer's choice. It provides an understanding of the motives for a potential customer to choose the brand or detects barriers that cause the consumer to drop out of the buying process. This helps the team adopt strategies to overcome such barriers or ride on the opportunities they present.

The Brand Benefits: Conventional logic is to list out the benefits to a customer from a product perspective. However, as the team begins creating the brand strategy, a better and different understanding of the consumer and their expectations from the brand could emerge. This is often a revelation to teams as they begin to appreciate those aspects of the product, which the consumers find useful and therefore need to be highlighted in communication.

Convincing Support for the Brand's Claim: These are the reasons why the consumers should believe a brand's promise. They constitute the magic recipe or secret sauce that lends credibility to a brand's claim. These could be tangible or intangible, but in both cases, they have to be true.

The Brand Personality: Defines the tone of the brand. Depending on the topic and consumer sensibilities, the brand must choose its tone of communication. This way, consumers begin associating the brand with a particular character and identity that is unique and distinct, aiding the transmission of information smoothly and successfully.

The Brand Differentiator: This is the brand's proposition—the elevator pitch that convinces the consumer to select the brand over others—the compelling and competitive reason for the consumer to choose the brand. It could be either a rational or an emotional reason or a combination of both. But that, which has to be different from every other competitor's proposition. It needs to be articulated in an inspiring and powerful manner in order to encourage the customer to act in favor of the brand.

The Brand Mission: While consumers choose brands for their unique selling propositions, it is the brand's mission that creates empathy and warmth in the relationship between the brand and the consumer. It elevates the relationship from transactional to one of constant engagement. Consumers look up and follow such brands, believing them to be leaders, creating a better world for all, in the long run.

In my career, I have often come across entrepreneurs and founders of start-ups who have told me that building a company or product brand was not a priority for them. On probing, most of them have a common set of reasons to give.

First, they believe that brand building is for "big companies" especially for companies that have consumer brands. "You know, we aren't P&G or Amazon or Apple or even Uber. We're a B2B company. We make things that are bought by company personnel and we mostly deal with the commercial department where only price works! If you want to benchmark us, treat us like Accenture or Oracle or FedEx or Siemens or LinkedIn."

It's only when it is pointed out that all the brands mentioned command a premium that the nickel drops. These companies are in fact, often the first choice of their customers even when there are cheaper options available from smaller lesser-known companies.

Why is it so? Answer is, the assurance of getting a quality product and service. The confidence that in the unlikely event of something going wrong, there would be a quick and effective response to tackle all issues and resolve the matter at the earliest. This reassurance is the intangible value for the customer, which no reduction in price can equal. The premium that customers gladly pay for this assurance is the power and value of the brand, built over decades of delivering quality products and services.

Brand building and the creation of brand value is not about advertising and communication only. It is a combination of many factors that includes, but is not restricted to advertising and communication. Powerful brands leverage all aspects of brand building *including* advertising and communication to build their brand. Which is why, no amount of advertising can propel a brand with a weak proposition or service delivery or product experience or any other critical aspect of brand building, to success. The difference between consumer brands and B2B brands is that consumer brands rely a bit more on advertising and communication, whereas B2B brands rely a bit less on these, for success. But all brands need the right mix of everything to be successful in business.

Clients owning consumer-facing brands never tire to remind me,

> Our products are bought by dealers or distributors or purchase intermediaries. These guys are only keen on the margins they earn. As long as we provide them with hefty margins, we are good. The end consumer totally trusts the trade.

A similar argument is also put forth by companies that operate in consumer sectors with strong intermediaries such as construction, building materials, décor, and so on. In this segment, the building contractor, architect, civil contractor, house painter, interior decorator, plumber, electrical contractor and electrician play important influencer roles. This is also true when it comes to business machinery, IT systems and software purchase among others. Here consultants are important influencers. "They have the veto power." I'm often told.

Nothing could be worse for your brand than letting third parties decide its fate. The intermediaries will take your attractive margin and stock your product as long as there's genuine consumer demand. Remember, like everyone else, they too want to sell more with minimum effort. If they can sell three competitor products at the same time that they take to sell one of yours, why would they spend more time selling you even if you give a 20 percent higher margin per product? Don't blame them, anyone would do the same. So, the best way to get intermediaries on your side is to create powerful demand for your brand, such that you actually are in a position to pay less margin to your dealer!

On the other hand, strong brands instill confidence among consumers even when powerful influencers and intermediaries exist. These brands often tackle the issues that influencers and intermediaries can raise by engaging directly with the end user. While these intermediaries can eliminate weak brands with their veto power, they won't want to put their relationship with the end customer on line by speaking up too loudly against powerful brands and soon, end up toeing the line. Check it out for yourself, 90 percent of influencers and intermediaries inevitably recommend market leaders. It puts them in a safe place, because in case of any issues they simply remind you that they recommended the best in the category.

So, banish from your mind, any restrictions about the kind of business you are in, the people you sell to, the channels you work with and focus your efforts in building a great experience for everyone who encounters your brand. This positive experience is the intangible value that consumers, intermediaries, partners and employees will attach with your brand. These positive experiences are what bring customers back. That's why, it's called *goodwill*. This sentiment is the primary reason consumers choose your brand over competition, happily paying a premium for it.

The other common excuse I've heard from start-up founders is:

I know I have to build a brand, but that's not our priority today. Brand building is for the long term you see and we're a startup, we have to justify our investors' faith in us. We can't be blowing their money on brand building. We have to show that we're selling and meet their business matrices. We aren't profitable yet and we need to start showing profits.

Indeed, shareholders and investors' money should be the most important concern of not just a start-up, but of all business managers. But simply worrying about it and thinking narrowly in terms of month on month and quarter after quarter is not going to solve the problem. You might squeeze out a few extra bucks here and there but this strategy is not sustainable. If you truly value investor money, then your plan must be to return it with a healthy margin over a sustained period of time. While a short-term focus is needed for the initial months, it may end up being detrimental to your business if stretched beyond that.

What is going to help you provide sustained returns to your investors is, building value into your offerings. This value is the buffer that gets reflected in your company's balance sheet. Your brand equity is what helps you attract the best talent and keeps them motivated at work. This becomes your unique offering to your customer who willingly pays more for a better experience strengthening your bottom line. In this manner, not only do you return your investors' money but you also increase the value of your own stake retaining control of the company you founded.

Your customers will always let you know about the value your brand delivers, through feedback and repeat purchases. These comments are highly valued in most boardroom meetings, for they bring to life, the role the brand plays in the consumer's life. Even if the financial results aren't good, positive customer reviews often save the day for many a start-up, because investors realize the potential in those customer reviews.

So, from right *now* is a good time to start building your brand. Brand building is not just advertising, it's connecting everything from company vision, culture, product creation, customer engagement, service delivery and interactions, with a positive customer experience. Once you are freed from the thought that brand building is only advertising, you will begin to relook at your brand from the customer's point of view and develop a number of ways to enrich the customer's experience.

Having defined your customer well, examine your customer's journey, understand how they engage with the category and with your competition. What are the highlights that you can learn from? What are the mistakes being made that you can avoid? Are there any gaps for you to exploit? Now juxtapose your brand in the customer's journey and understand the difference. If there aren't any significant differences, you would know why, despite your best efforts, your financial performance is lackluster. Unless somewhere and somehow your brand makes a significant difference to the consumer in the journey, eventually you are going to run out of money and investors.

All this may still seem distant and not relevant for your current situation. As entrepreneurs, you may argue that brand building takes resources and time, both of which you have a paucity of. Perhaps this sounds like something you have heard of before and even attempted in the past, without success.

However, there is good news for you.

Advancements in science and technology have enabled us to relook at the process of brand building in a new light. Today, technology offers us opportunities that were not available to us in the past. Rapid advancements in computing power over the last decade has turned many technology concepts and theories into realities that we can actually work with today. The best part is that, a lot of those advancements can be applied to the effort of brand-building activities. So, set all your concerns aside and begin the process of developing a sound brand strategy, because now you have the power of technology on your side.

Having a well-defined brand strategy in place, is half the battle won. The next step is to translate this strategy into a well-executed plan. And here is where the next element of my book comes into play.

Artificial Intelligence (AI)

Most people are intimidated by the word. It brings to mind stories about rogue AI programs that began talking to each other without being told to do so, or of those that mastered chess in merely four hours and others that learnt the complex Chinese mind game of Go so well as to beat its human champion, a feat once considered impossible.

These incidents become the fuel that inspires authors and screen writers to create stories forming an entire genre of entertainment referred to as "the AI Takeover" in our popular culture. Hollywood movies convert these outlandish concepts into postapocalyptic tales in which evil and malfunctioning AI programs trigger many a destructive spree that end entire civilizations and disrupt the relatively peaceful life we lead today. Presented and explained in a simple and lucid style that is supported with cutting-edge special effects, makes it easy for ordinary folk to consume, believe in and fear the destructive nature of AI.

It's important at this juncture to understand the symbiotic relation-ship pop fiction has shared with science. While sci-fi movies and books are flights of fancy, some of them actually turn out to be quite accurate in their conceptual thought. The three laws of robotics were actually written by popular sci-fi author Isaac Asimov in his 1942 short story "Runaround" and while they are a work of science fiction, they do find credibility in the world of robotics. From the visionary genius Leonardo DaVinci and early sci-fi writers such as Jules Verne and HG Wells to Hollywood movies, many items described and depicted in sci-fi such as AI, bionic hands, holograms and driverless cars have turned out into products that are find-ing applications today.

While pop culture continues to influence the perspective of a lot of people, a lot of common people also believe that AI is a distant concept and is not really connected to their lives. To many others it brings to mind the possibilities of exciting products such as self-driving cars and drones that deliver products to our doorsteps.

Reality is that AI has already entered our lives innocuously and in fact many of us, digital netizens encounter it in our daily activities, often unaware that we are using it to meet our everyday needs.

When your favorite grocery app presents you with daily deals that seem to reflect exactly what you were looking for, it's not a coincidence. Neither is it similar to what your neighbors receive on their screens from the very same app at that very same moment. This unique customization based on your needs and past buying behavior is an example of AI at work. When you tune in to your favorite OTT (Over The Top) network to watch a movie, the choice of movies and shows on offer for you is uniquely designed to suit your taste based on your viewing history, once again curated by AI. The news feeds on your social media channels, the videos that pop up when you browse YouTube, the sports news that pep-per your information sources and the products that populate the ecom-merce portal you visited, everything around you in your digital world, is there for a reason.

They have appeared because you showed interest, read about, researched, followed, commented about, reviewed, or evaluated something related to those categories online. And somewhere all of this has been understood by different AI programs that have begun to profile you and extrapolate your interests based on that profile, surrounding your online world with products, news, movies and other things that you are interested in.

Even if you hadn't done some of those activities to record your interest, based on your profile, AI systems today have the ability to match you with other people of a similar profile and use that likeness to generate a list of things you could possibly be interested in and offer it to you as you traverse the virtual world. Click on it and reinforce the stereotype or cross it, to create a new profile bucket, any action you take, only helps the AI learn more about you and improve its offering to you, the next time you come online.

So, AI isn't a distant concept, it's here and a part of our lives, enabling us to make better choices. In fact, every time you search on Google, AI comes into play, understanding you better and throwing up accurate suggestions based on learnings. You would have also noticed that as you search on Google, you encounter ads that are relevant to your search, on top of your search results or displayed on the side as you scroll down. Then as you continue browsing, the ads continue to follow you, displaying products and services that are relevant to your search or other aspects you may not have been actively searching for.

This brings us to an interesting observation. It demonstrates how well AI is entrenched into a key aspect of brand building—digital advertising. A 2019 survey by Salesforce indicates that over 51 percent marketers are already using AI and another 25 percent are well on their way to adopting AI in their marketing plans.

The reason why AI is rapidly finding adoption in marketing and advertising is because of the following reasons:

Targeting

As opposed to traditional media, which operated on a scatter-gun philosophy of targeting widely with a high amount of wastage, AI enables brands to be highly focused in their targeting on digital platforms. AI ensures your ads are being served to the right audience, who are seeking your product or have an affinity for your product category.

Measurement

Traditional media only offers broad measurement parameters such as readership figures for magazines or viewership numbers for television programs. These measurements could never tell you how many actually read your ad or viewed your commercial or went through your brochure or leaflet. They tended to club all kinds of ads together, providing you with only broad figures and a general understanding. With such broad numbers, marketers were never sure if a full-page ad on the third page was more effective than a quarter-page solus ad on the front page, or if a single 30-second advertisement was more effective than three 10-second spots on the same program. The huge investments made in celebrity endorsements could never be correlated with an improvement in brand perceptions, nor could any feedback be obtained through associations or sponsorship of events. With AI on the other hand, brands are completely aware of how many viewers saw their video through to the end, how many acted on their ads and what kind of customer reactions were got through a particular influencer activity.

Engagement

Traditional media is a one-way street in which brands send out their messages, hoping that consumers have seen it in its entirety and have understood its minute details. Owing to the prohibitive cost of traditional media, such one-way communication too was restricted to certain time periods of the year, day, month, or for festivals when the consumer was considered to be positively disposed to purchasing the brand or the product category. This actually created a seasonality for purchase, which few brands had the courage to break out of. In India for example, the festival of Diwali is considered to be a "fifth season" because almost a fifth of all consumer-durable purchase happens in the week of Diwali festivities. With limited media bandwidth and every brand paying top-dollar in trying to shout their message aloud, this behavior only increased the clutter in the period, leading to customer fatigue. Unfortunately, for a number of brands with lower budgets, their messages are often drowned out in the deafening noise, wasting a lot of marketing resource and effort. Slogan-writing contests have been traditionally treated as customer response and the few letters that customers sent in were considered the gold-standard in direct marketing. This entire landscape has undergone a sea of change. Today AI-driven chatbots can provide a 24×7 interface with clients. Brands can engage with customers on a daily basis, understand their expectations better and make suggestions accordingly.

Prediction

Marketing companies traditionally invest huge sums in product development and consumer research to understand what their customers want from the product categories. Today AI can help brands predict consumer behavior with great accuracy. The kind of vehicles customers desire, trending colors of the season, travel destinations, movie genres and even food preferences, everything can be gathered with a high percentage of accuracy. All of this is gleaned from the humongous amounts of data that consumers willingly share online. With all this information, AI can help brands, augment, fine-tune, conceive and assemble its range to meet the expectations of the consumer with a great degree of precision.

Today, AI applications cut across many spheres of digital marketing and its use is spreading deeper and wider in the domain. As the AI improves its learning and provides better customer experiences, more application areas emerge and this process is one of continuous improvement. Some of the most common areas in digital marketing where AI is used are:

Content Generation: AI tools can create content based on keywords provided. While these may not yet match up to a human's creative writing abilities, they are sufficiently good in creating interest and grabbing attention of the customer in a quick and cost-efficient manner.

Email Marketing: Gone are the days of having to buy dubious mailing lists, through automation and AI suites, brands can build their own rich database and ensure the right mails are sent to different consumers creating a highly effective communication mechanism.

Advertising: AI-driven advertising tools help brands target the right audience and build effective engagement online.

Customer Support: Chatbots predict consumer sentiment and proactively provide information to consumers and automatically escalate the matter when required.

Website Development: Now brands can create responsive website designs using AI that develop designs based on an iterative learning process.

User Experience: Predictive AI tools enable brands to provide their customers with a customized user experience.

Augmented Reality (AR): Integrating AR with AI takes the consumer experience to a whole new level. First, the sensorial experience it provides customers is truly out-of-the-world. Then there's a tangible benefit too, especially relevant in the times of a pandemic when social-distancing norms become prevalent. In this, brands can provide remote product and tech support by combining AR with AI.

I trust you have understood well, the importance of building brands and how it creates value. You would have also got a primer on how AI is affecting our lives and how it is driving digital advertising. In the following chapters, we will attempt to use the advances happening in the world of AI to help entrepreneurs and business managers in the process of building brands and creating huge value for their owners.

Chapter Summary

1. Brands offer customers a unique combination of rational and emotional benefits. Consumers choose brands based on this unique set of benefits, often willing to pay a premium for it.
2. Brand-building activities create value for an organization over a period of time. This brand value is often worth many times the value of the company's physical assets.
3. Brand building begins by creating a distinct brand strategy that defines all the critical aspects of the brand: Source of growth, audience definition, customer insight, brand benefits, brand supports, brand personality, brand differentiator and finally the brand mission.
4. Brand-building efforts need to begin from the first day of a company's existence.
5. Brand building is not just advertising, it is about creating engaging and unique journeys for customers and stakeholders.
6. Computing power has unleashed a technological revolution today, turning AI concepts into actual applications we use in our daily lives.
7. Advertising is one area where AI is widely used and applied across the world.
8. AI has changed the paradigm in brand building because it is targeted, measurable, engaging and predictive.
9. Today AI is used in various aspects of digital marketing, including content generation, email marketing, advertising, customer support, website development, user experience and augmented reality.
10. AI can be used effectively in different areas of brand-building activity and helps in the creation of brand value without the inefficiencies of traditional models.

CHAPTER 2

Overview

The previous chapter presented the case for brand building, outlined the process for developing a brand strategy and examined the increasing importance of AI. This chapter underlines the impact that brands have in the lives of their consumers and the resultant effect on its valuations. It details the process of creating a robust brand architecture.

- Conducting a brand workshop: the complete process.
- Brand Strategy Document, a must for ensuring the successful implementation of the brand strategy.
- Setting brand objectives using the Consumer Purchase Journey.

Brand, a Guarantee of Value

According to the BrandZ Top 100 Most Valuable Global Brands 2020 ranking, Amazon, the U.S.-based e-commerce giant is the world's most valued brand with a value of over $415 billion. Amazon's annual revenue in 2019 was $280.552 billion. Imagine that the value of its brand is 1.48 times the total revenue that the company generated for that whole year! That's the worth of the goodwill the brand has generated over the past few years by providing us with a fantastic experience on the site, following that up with great offers, friendly interface, excellent support, unmatched convenience, regular feedback and reward programs.

But the impact of Amazon goes beyond the realms of providing great service. Amazon has done a unique thing—it has changed or modified consumer behavior permanently and that too around the world. Today, we can't imagine the world without Amazon or e-commerce. If Amazon wasn't there tomorrow, a whole lot of us would be stumped for some time, thinking of alternatives. Amazon has not just elevated our lifestyles; it has forced the entire e-commerce ecosystem to step up. Amazon pushes itself and also pushes its smaller and nimbler competitors to innovate and match Amazon in their offerings. A good number of those competitors have smartly segmented the categories and many of them even lead Amazon in some categories. Much to the benefit of us, consumers.

Amazon has not just impacted our shopping behavior, but through its other products such as Prime and Amazon Web Services (AWS), has evolved into a multidimensional brand that pushes the boundaries of innovation in various facets of the consumer's life, be it work or entertainment. Indeed, Amazon is well deserving of its stupendous brand value that has factored into it, the sum total of the goodwill and positive sentiments the consumer holds for the brand, which revenue figures alone cannot capture adequately. This is a great example of brand value creation. As entrepreneurs and business managers, we must keep Amazon and similar value creators as benchmarks and through the use of technology and innovation, aim to create an unparalleled brand experience for our customers. The net result should be such that in the absence of our brand, customers should express sentiments of feeling alone and lost. Such impactful experiences and purposeful brands are what lead change, creating enormous brand value that can be monetized.

Amazon is one example, the same report assigns Apple at the No. 2 position with a brand value of over $352 billion against total net sales of $260.17 billion in FY 2019, followed by Microsoft valued at over $326 billion against an annual revenue of more than $125 billion in 2019, Google at over $323 billion (annual 2019 revenue $161.9 billion) and VISA at the fifth position with a brand value of over $186 billion (annual 2019 revenue $9.7 billion).

It is important to note that three of the top five companies are relatively young brands with Google and Amazon categorized as being companies of the current century. This information is both revealing and inspiring. It tells you that brand building isn't difficult. Nor is it a function of age. You can be a young company, yet create enormous brand value. That's because brand value is not a function of how much money you spend in the media, but of how great a difference you bring to the consumer's life.

Bring an enormous difference to the consumer, provide them with conveniences, reduce their inefficiencies, make their lives easier, simpler, richer and then, keep working on it continuously and the consumer will value your effort. They will perceive the genuineness of your intentions, understand the purpose behind your vision and appreciate the thought that you apply to the seemingly small details of their lives. In turn the consumer will reward you with their loyalty, which would be worth many times the effort you put in.

So, brand building will lead to brand value creation, which is more than the effort that will go into it. Brands actually multiply an organization's worth. Think of it as a philosophy guiding your operations. While your business operations will return you profits, this philosophy will also connect with your customers who will reward you for it, multiplying the overall worth of your enterprise.

Building a brand begins with developing a good brand strategy. In the previous chapter, I have outlined the critical elements that constitute a brand strategy. As a first step get down to writing them down. If you don't have a background in marketing or advertising, you may find it daunting. My suggestion for you is not to try doing this alone. Developing your brand strategy should be a group endeavor. Ideally do this at an offsite workshop. Use an external moderator who can impartially guide your team through the process. It will bring focus and commitment to the process.

Here are some guidelines on how to conduct an effective brand strategy workshop.

Who Should Attend?

The company management as well as key business decision makers have to be a part of this effort. Also, those responsible for carrying forward the strategy, that is the marketing and operations team are required to compulsorily attend the workshop. It is important that attendees devote their attention to the workshop and are not distracted by calls or other matters during the workshop. Attendees must be contributors. There is little point in having silent participants, therefore it is advisable not to include them, allowing them to put their time to better use. With this perspective, it is best to restrict the participants to a maximum of 15 members.

Create a Background

Prior to conducting a workshop, the practice is to circulate a background document—a single sheeter that captures the current situation of the company and outlines the aim of the workshop. The purpose of doing this is to capture the viewpoints of all key stakeholders and align participants to a common platform. Thus, ensuring all participants at the start of the workshop are already at an agreement on the current situation with a budding perspective for the future, creating the ground for constructive discussion and debate during the workshop. The document is a consolidation of the views of the participants and forms the perfect backdrop for the workshop. The background note should succinctly capture details of the four key determinants of a good strategy: Industry Overview, Competitive Framework, Company Situation and the Consumer Perspective.

Ideally, the note should be circulated a week in advance of the workshop and participants must be encouraged to read and familiarize themselves with the perspective captured in the document so that no time is wasted during the workshop, in bringing participants to a common understanding of the task at hand.

Conducting the Workshop

At the workshop, participants must debate and discuss the key elements that make up the foundation of the brand strategy. The process should ideally be structured and moderated by an external member, proficient in conducting brand workshops along the format suggested in the earlier chapter. This should lead to a rich discussion in which participants present their views that are then reviewed and debated at length before concluding on the most relevant fit.

Similar processes have been used extensively by leading companies globally, enabling them to create some of the biggest consumer and business brands in the world. The strength of this process lies in its ability to guide the participants through healthy debate and discussion to develop a unique perspective of the situation. Eventually, distilling and refining their collective wisdom into an enduring vision and direction for the brand going forward.

Steps Following the Brand Workshop

The brand workshop will align all members to a common objective outlined in the strategy document. This will provide a clear direction on what exactly needs to be communicated to whom. The output from the workshop is to be collated, crafted and polished and shared by mail with all attendees. Their suggestions will be incorporated and the final output will become the BRAND STRATEGY DOCUMENT, which will be the input for development of marketing plans, creative communication and outreach programs.

This common understanding and agreement will need to be followed up with a deep dive to outline the specific activities and plans to meet the stated objectives captured in the strategy document. This will form the nucleus of the program leading to the creation of a strong identity for the brand, along with developing a narrative that can help customers connect with the brand.

There are many alternative tools and techniques also available to develop a brand strategy. While some are basic, others are more elaborate. Do go through a few and select the one that you understand well and feel most comfortable with. There's one more important aspect to the exercise. When you're creating your brand strategy, keep your business hat aside and make sure that your team members do the same. A brand creation exercise should be done with an open mind, without tinting the effort with functional biases. Having conducted many such exercises, I have realized that the ones in which participants kept aside their biases and allowed their minds to freely discuss all possibilities, have been the most successful ones. On the other hand, exercises in which participants held their cards close to their chests and tried to influence the outcome have always proven to be ineffective. It's also a sad waste of time and resource. What is the point of spending money and time in conducting a brand workshop if your objective is never to build one?

It's actually quite simple; if you continue to do the same thing, you're never going to be able to explore new opportunities. Developing a brand strategy through such an exercise allows people to lower their guards and see the situation from their customer's perspective. This opens up a world of possibilities as ideas flow freely. Ideas from one participant are often developed by the others in the group and eventually culminate into a huge opportunity that none thought existed. So often have I observed this happening: A young intern may have a seemingly strange idea that catches the attention of a senior colleague who appreciates its possibilities, a tech person then picks up one of those possibilities and explains how it can be worked out and soon ideas begin flowing freely in a frenzy with everyone contributing and before you know it, the company has developed a whole new perspective on engaging with their consumers!

In this manner brands are born.

A lot of entrepreneurs and business managers hesitate to initiate the first step. They hold back saying, "We don't have the money to do consumer research, to know what our customers are looking for." Or, "We really haven't thought about the competition or about our product. It's all still evolving."

The truth is no product is ever fully ready. All products have to keep evolving. Simply because the consumer is evolving! But brands are NOT products. Brands too have to evolve but their trajectory has to be different. Brands LEAD customers in their behavior, habit and thinking and not the other way round. Great brands imagine the world, *before it becomes that way*. In other words, great brands are like great statesmen, visionaries, inventors and artists, they are able to conjure up a better world. This ability is what makes brands endearing to customers. Don't worry if your product is evolving. Your brand's growth and development can begin alongside and guess what? Your brand's vision can actually lead product development.

As far as consumer research is concerned, it's great if you have it handy. Today, it's not too difficult to constitute one. Keep in mind that not all researches need a research agency. You can conduct a quick research online on survey tools such as Survey Monkey and get a good idea of the direction the consumer wants to take, in a matter of days. You could also simply pick up the phone and speak to your customers. If 10 of your team members talk to 20 people each, you would have collectively spoken to 200 people, which is a fairly decent sample size to provide you with a direction. That should give you a lot of confidence in understanding what's going on in your customer's mind.

Sometimes, you may not need to do research. I have experienced that most entrepreneurs and many business managers have an extremely good understanding of their customers. This happens with the experience of dealing with customers, day in and out. Few researches can equal that learning. While some managers and entrepreneurs are sensitive and naturally adept at decoding and categorizing conversations as consumer feedback, others are not so and are slow to make the connection. While they may have registered and also acted upon feedback, they haven't learnt the ability to cluster and categorize it in the form of a learning process. The feedback remains restricted in their minds and in their subconscious. Conducting a brand strategy exercise helps release this rich information in a fertile environment among the right talent, who build upon it to create powerful brand stories.

This process helps put your brand strategy in place. The brand strategy becomes your guiding document to begin developing your brand plan, or to audit the current brand plan. Here's a list of some of the more important brand properties you need to create/audit in the first stage of your brand plan, based on this strategy document.

1. Brand Name.
2. Logo.
3. Brand's proposition to the customer.
4. Product design.
5. Consumer journey and experience.
6. All first-level communication collateral encountered by the consumer, that is, product literature, user manual and so on.
7. Brand primary and secondary packaging.
8. Website and social media presence.
9. Tone of communication.
10. Workspace design and communication to internal audience.
11. Communication to trade.
12. Retail experience and visibility elements, for example, shop signages, in-shop communication.
13. Label designs, stationery design, associated elements design.
14. Digital and offline communication. Here, you must create a visual and copy guideline manual that captures the detail of the execution elements.
15. Associations and affiliate marketing programs.
16. Brand sponsorships.
17. Celebrity endorsements.
18. Service Standard Operating Procedures (SOPs) and guidelines.
19. Customer interaction modes and manuals.
20. Events, exhibitions and trade activations.

Once you have this in place, conduct the same exercise for the other brands in your company portfolio. Evaluate the role of sub-brands and variants as well. If any of them appear weak, this is the right time to either do away with them altogether, or merge them into the mother brand or a sub or a variant of the brand.

Having completed this exercise, you must now document all aspects of it. The document that will encapsulate this effort is called the **Brand Architecture Document** or **BAD**.

This document is either a physical one that you can have copies made of and distributed to all offices around the world, or it could be a soft copy to be e-mailed, or uploaded on an intranet site, accessible only on a need-to-know basis through a login ID and password. The advantage of making it available online is that you can keep adding, appending, improvising it over time. Each time an update happens, an automated e-mail gets triggered to the relevant people globally keeping them abreast of developments in real time.

The BAD must be comprehensive to include all the properties listed earlier. Wherever possible, it must be illustrated with examples and samples, down to its finest details. Take the logo for example, it must contain the specific CMYK (Cyan, Magenta, Yellow, and Key or Black, which are the colors used in the printing process) and RGB (Red, Green and Blue. RGB is the color scheme associated with electronic displays) numbers of the colors used in the logo. These standards specify the unique color of the logo. By specifying the color, you are ensuring that your logo is reproduced identically on a visiting card in India and on an exhibition panel in Australia. The BAD also specifies how the logo should be used on different substrates and different color backgrounds and more importantly highlights how it SHOULD NOT be used. It indicates the minimum size that the logo can appear in and also how it should be used along with other logos in various other applications.

In short, it's a dummy's guide for representing your brand. By creating it, you are eliminating ambiguity and misinterpretation forever. The BAD ensures that the brand's vision, proposition, identity and experience is captured in a water-tight document that simply needs to be followed to provide the exact same brand experience, everywhere in the world.

Don't think of this task as being tedious, neither is it something that should be delegated to a junior team member. It is completely and totally the responsibility of the brand owner to develop the BAD. The only other people you can entrust the task with are the set who were involved in the brand workshop. Remember, delegation without proper briefing could have disastrous consequences. Any loss in translation is like a virus in this system that will snowball into a maze of confusion. You will have only yourself to blame, if months later, when reviewing the results of execution, you discover to your shock that the clear vision of the brand strategy has been watered-down to a weak version of that glorious start.

The BAD is very often the reason why brands succeed or fail. Powerful brands have a clear and distinct identity that is uniformly executed with precision in every part of the world. Which is why a brand like DHL conjures up the same set of images to all of us. That unique slanting red and yellow logo, the yellow and red airplanes, vans and t-shirts of the delivery personnel. The experience of the call center, the website and the office. The airway bill that you receive. The detailed debriefing you receive at the time of handing over the package articulating when the package will be shipped and when it is likely to arrive at the destination. Who you can call and how you can check the progress. Here is a brand that is providing you with a uniquely consistent and reassuring experience. Contrast that with a delivery experience you may have had with a local service that went horribly wrong. Chances are you may not even recall the logo of that logistics company. Post that bad experience, every time you walk into or encounter DHL, you can't help but feel a sense of reassurance.

That is how a brand delivers a complete experience.

With the creation and execution of the BAD, you have defined the brand and the customer experience it delivers. However, your task is still not done. You still have to set your brand objectives for the current period.

To do this, you must place yourself once again in the customer's shoes and walk through the Customer Purchase Journey. A Purchase Journey is about plotting the entire cycle that a customer goes through in the product category your brand operates in. A Purchase Journey typically begins from the moment when the customer realizes he needs to purchase the product and ends with the customer's postpurchase behavior. A typical Purchase Journey would have the following steps:

Realization

This is the stage when the customer first feels the need. This stage identifies and enumerates all the events that trigger the category-felt need. Powerful brands often own categories and sometimes are category creators. For example, in India, Maggi 2-minute noodles created and owns the 4 to 6 p.m. mini-meal category, so much so that it's not uncommon for mothers across India to ask their children in the evenings, "Hungry? should I make you a Maggi?" Understanding triggers is very important for brands because it clarifies how, when and where consumers enter a category. Using this information, brands can connect with consumer motivations and category drivers such as pain points, time of the year, seasonality, occasion, peer or family pressure and so on.

Search

This is the stage when a customer is actively searching for options to solve their need. In examining this stage, brand owners will understand the steps that consumers take to find a solution: What are the considered options? Do they search on Google? If so, what are the common key words? How do they structure their search queries? Which sites do they visit? Whose opinions matter?

Obviously, brands that tick all boxes have a better chance of making the cut. The important thing for a brand custodian is to find out how many of those boxes is their brand ticking off. This exercise will illuminate the entire search process and will highlight the brand's absence or the strength of its presence in the relevant places. If the brand team have been complaining in the past about lack of awareness, chances are that this audit will point out if the brand is present at all, in the places where the customer is conducting the search.

Evaluation

Now the customer is deep in the process of evaluating different options. Imagine them as having different travel sites open in different tabs of their web browsers. They're switching between tabs, checking out the hotels, rooms and their features on offer, or evaluating different airlines, prices, travel time and value additions. At this stage, the customer is looking to extract the best value for themselves. Here, well-positioned offers will swing the deal. Does the brand have a book now pay later option? Has the brand tied up with a popular credit card that's giving heftier discounts? Is the brand providing a full refund policy or a meal? In such situations, dynamic and lucrative offers will swing the decision in the brand's favor.

Usage

This is the act of consumption. The moment of truth for the brand. This could be a mundane activity that the customer could undertake without much thought, like using a bar of soap or toothpaste or an involved moment like a travel destination, a music app, a perfume or fashionwear. Just because the brand is involved in a habitual task, it does not mean that the brand isn't put to test. It's merely that the test of promise happens later. If the brand of soap or toothpaste doesn't deliver on its promise, they're going to be replaced very soon. When the experience is an involved one, the sensorial and emotional feel of the brand experience is very important. Did the brand just deliver a high point in the customer's life? Did it empower the customer to shine? Did the brand make the customer feel wonderful about themselves? If yes, the brand may have ensured a powerful connection for life.

Conversation

A memorable experience often stands out when customers make comparisons among the experiences they've had. If your brand has had a hand in delivering a memorable vacation, chances are that you will be their first choice for the next vacation. What's more, it's highly likely that your brand would have been mentioned in their conversations with friends and on social media sites. Brands that enrich moments in the consumer's life can be assured that those valuable moments featuring the brand will be mentioned many times again, in different conversations over time. Unfortunately, the same can be expected to befall brands that fail their customers.

A realistically created Purchase Journey will highlight the key decision points in the consumer's path to purchase. You will get insights into recognizing important triggers. It will also throw up customer pain points and issues that are not being currently addressed. It will provide you with the ability to map where your brand features in the Purchase Journey, how, why and where it gets chosen or eliminated and the critical reasons for the same.

Creating the journey will provide directions and insights into areas that the brand needs to concentrate on building. At what point on the journey is the customer most inclined to consider you, what could be a suitably compelling message at that point and what channels are most conducive to delivering that message.

On completing this process, you would have successfully translated your brand vision into a working plan that focuses your efforts on winning you maximum customers.

Chapter Summary

1. Brands are valued at many times their operating annual turnover. This worth is not a function of the age of the brand. It is valued based on the positive change the brand brings to a consumer's life.

2. Valuable brands improve the lives of customers often by changing habit, behavior and providing huge benefits such as convenience, saving and so on.

3. Building great value begins by creating a powerful brand strategy.

4. A good strategy can be developed by involving key stakeholders and conducting a brand strategy workshop.

5. The output of the brand strategy workshop becomes the input for developing the Brand Architecture Document (BAD), which details out the 20 key elements of brand communication.

6. Creation of the BAD is the responsibility of the key stakeholders. This task cannot be delegated.

7. The BAD is the guiding document for the brand, eliminating subjectivity in brand communication. It ensures uniformity of design, experience, presentation and tone. The BAD is made accessible to all members tasked with executing the brand plan and is to be strictly adhered to.

8. Next step is to determine the brand's immediate objectives.

9. Conducting an audit of the Customer Purchase Journey will highlight the critical brand tasks to tackle in the immediate term.

10. The Customer Purchase Journey comprises of five stages: Realization, Search, Evaluation, Usage and Conversation. Auditing this journey will help a brand to understand which part of the journey to focus on, the message to convey and the medium to use in order to achieve the objective.

CHAPTER 3

Overview

Previous chapters have underscored the importance of brand building and presented the process for developing a sound brand strategy. This chapter examines the rise of AI and how it has permeated many areas of modern living.

- Instances of humans directly talking to machines.
- Computing power: The reason for the rise of AI in recent times.
- Understanding the context: when machines made the leap.
- Definition of AI and ML.
- How AI learns today.
- The opportunity that AI provides for young brands.
- What AI can and what it can't do for brands.
- How AI improves efficiencies.
- Why AI will become all-pervasive in the future.
- The requirements for AI to succeed.
- Shortcomings of AI.
- Supervised and Unsupervised learning.
- How AI is different from human intelligence.

An Introduction to AI

The Indian Institute of Technology (IIT), Joint Entrance Exam (JEE) are hugely important to millions of Indian students, aspiring to obtain globally lauded engineering degrees from these prestigious institutes. Graduating from these institutes assures a student of gaining employment with the best companies in India and the world, at salaries that are astronomically higher than what average Indians can ever hope to earn in their lifetimes. No wonder many are willing to cheat and pay hundreds of thousands of rupees to clear the examination. This has led to a proliferation of racketeers who use the most dubious and ingenious of methods to assure admission for students willing to shell out huge amounts of cash. One common trick is to recruit needy students who have successfully cleared the exam in the past few years to take the exam on behalf of their undeserving clients. But this year, thanks to a unique AI algorithm, the National Testing Agency was able to identify 56 impersonators whose faces matched with top-ranked candidates from the previous two years. This information would be shared with all institutes preventing their admission thus ensuring only deserving students get their due. AI is beneficial to one and all and while instances such as the one described is happening at one end of the world, AI is now an integral part of our lives, perhaps even more than we may realize.

A unique thing has happened of late. Humans have begun to speak with machines. That's right. Some of us have done it a few times, others do it regularly and very soon, only a minority wouldn't have done it at all. It won't come as a surprise to you that the ones doing it regularly are the younger generation, our children. How many times have you been reminded by your child when you're keying in search terms on your phone, "Mom (or Dad) why don't you try Google Assist?" The first time they said that, you may have perhaps wondered what they were referring to, isn't it?

Well, you are not alone, the rapid pace and progress of technology is now a reality that's impacting our lives and improving it bit-by-bit almost every day. Once, computing power was expensive and its access was restricted to a select few—governments and large companies. This meant that while we read about the developments, or heard of them or even watched them, courtesy of a documentary, or during a visit to their facilities, it would take years, sometimes decades for that technology to get commercialized. Many years would pass before that technology could be sold, first to an elite audience and then as costs reduced with the passage of time, become accessible and affordable to the common man.

But today, we've crossed the tipping point when it comes to computing power. Watches, cycles and even shoes now have the ability to capture, store and analyze data. Today, we generate close to 3 quintillion bytes of data every day. Close to 60 percent of the world population are active internet users. Every day, Google processes over 5.6 billion search queries, 306.4 billion e-mails are sent, 500 million messages are tweeted each day, 8.95 million photos and videos are shared on Instagram per day and over 25 percent of the world's online population use Facebook. What is astonishing is that more than 90 percent of all the data existing in the world was created in the last 2 years alone! By 2025, humans will be generating more than 460 exabytes of data every day.

All this information is an indication of the democratization of computing power and flow of data and information. This has resulted in technologies improving at a rapid pace and today, these technologies touch us in seemingly innocuous ways in more aspects than we realize. Like Google Assist for example, which enables you to talk to your phone and to the internet. You may wonder what's so unique about talking to your phone? To you it might simply be a matter of convenience that's saving you the trouble of laboriously typing out your queries on the phone.

Well, it is not that simple, when you realize the technology that goes behind delivering this simple act of convenience. First, there is a perceivable difference between typing something out and speaking it aloud. In your mind you believe you are doing the same thing. However, on observing closely, you will notice that words intending to communicate the same phrase, emanate differently when spoken and when written.

This happens because when you are writing, you unconsciously make adjustments to accommodate the context of the written word. The same thing happens when you speak. But the context in both cases is different. In the case of the written word, you factor in a reader and try to ensure you leave no room for doubt. While you may actually modify your words even as you speak, improvising to the reaction of your audience. Which is why the same phrase is said differently, when spoken and when written to *mean the same thing*. And guess what? Google realizes and acknowledges this difference. Google's voice assist is now powered by AI, which understands the contextual difference between your textual and voice-based search and will throw up different search results that factor in the context of your written or spoken words.

You're not just talking to a machine. You are talking to an intelligent system that is capable of second guessing what you have in mind and what you are trying to communicate. It will accordingly dish out matching results. In a manner, the system is mimicking the way we humans think. It has the ability to not take you for the literal words that you've said or written, but to understand your query from the context and the background it places you in. It takes into account your geography, the phrases you're using and the medium you've used, to make an accurate judgment of what you could have in mind and then decide what you want from it. Which is why today, search results for the exact terms by the same person on different devices, locations and time of the day, will throw up different search results. Similarly, search results for different individuals at the same location using similar devices, will also throw up different search results.

AI now has the ability to put all the search terms in the right context and is personalizing the output, uniquely to what it believes you are seeking.

This behavior, the ability to put words and phrases in a context that fits the profile, device, usage of words and location of a person and then provide likely solutions, is exactly the way a human would behave. A good salesman at a retail outlet will first size you up, then ask you the right questions without appearing intrusive. Using this information and from his past experience, he then proceeds to help you find exactly what you are looking for. Similarly, if you had to meet a business associate for the first time for lunch, most likely you'd do a quick think up about the person and recommend a place and cuisine, which you think the person would be comfortable with. You do this by judging the available time, background, appearance and accent of the person, then combine that knowledge with the possible eateries close by and recommend the one that should fit the bill. Today, our phones do the same for us.

This ability of the system to behave and offer solutions *like* a human being is called Artificial Intelligence.

The process through which the system learns from behavior, usage, context, tone and reactions is Machine Learning.

These are the two important concepts that you'll need to keep in mind as you go through the rest of the book.

Currently, an entire ecosystem of different AI systems is learning from your online actions and behavior. From reading choices online, favorite sports, buying behavior, clothes, holiday preferences, friends, comments, background and so on, everything is being analyzed and categorized continuously to understand you better and match your needs with the right products and services, with the aim to make living easier and more convenient for you.

The previous chapter has detailed the process that needs to be followed in order to develop a unique brand strategy. Post that it had provided a structure to help understand the consumer's purchase journey and then underlined the steps for creating an immediate term plan aimed at achieving the stated objectives.

In short it encapsulates the "theoretical" portion of brand building.

From my experience, completing this theoretical process is something that 90 percent of brands fail to do. Next, putting this theoretical exercise into practical activities has proved to be daunting even for the most ardent believers of brand building. That's because this step brings the brand up against debilitating business realities. Resistance from well-entrenched competition and existing industry stakeholders to begin with. Then there is lack of support from traditional distribution channels, limited media avenues to reach out to consumers, restricted talent from a narrow pool of resources and an environment that severely restricts any scope for providing a better consumer experience. All put together, over the years, these factors have suffocated and strangled many a promising brand.

Unless brands had unlimited resources at their disposal, or a product innovation par excellence or an experience or value proposition that was unequivocally unique, it was difficult for brands to stand out and successfully compete in their categories. This cast iron template has proven to be indomitable, providing market leaders with a powerful leverage to maintain the status quo. Consequently, the experience of trying hard yet failing repeatedly is what eventually killed the belief in brand building among business owners and marketers.

But the rise of AI is an opportunity for young brands to bypass the traditional setup and create an alternative route to connect with the consumer. Today brands can plug into various intelligent systems that are creating substitute channels to reach customers, circumventing the traditional method of brand building. In fact, the biggest advantage to brands of today over their well-entrenched traditional competitor is the opportunity to leverage this AI-enabled parallel universe.

There's a caveat though. Having an AI-first approach to brand building does not mean that by simply pressing a button, AI will automatically do everything that it takes to dish out a highly valuable brand. It is also incorrect to expect that the AI is going to substitute strategic thinking for the brand. Neither is this a cheap and inexpensive way of building a brand. AI is simply a route—an alternate route that uses technology instead of traditional channels to build a brand. It will continue to require strategic thinking of the highest order and huge efforts on a continuous basis, to achieve success.

A brand strategy is a comprehensive document that will outline a clear path for you to build your brand and gain a competitive advantage for you, among your customers. However, today's environment is extremely fluid and dynamic, with new options for consumers emerging on a regular basis. In such a situation, it is critical that you are constantly reviewing your brand strategy and plan. Strategy reviews must take place on a quarterly basis if not monthly, and plans must be evaluated for their efficiencies on a monthly, if not weekly basis. You have to continuously monitor your competition, the consumer and the environment for signs of change and adapt your course accordingly. Stakeholders have to be continually evaluating future strategies, for AI cannot do such a broad spectrum of tasks as yet.

AI is a technological advancement, unique to our current times, which you can deploy to gain a competitive advantage for your brand and achieve your brand objectives. AI is an alternative *means* to execute your brand-building plans as opposed to the traditional method of brand building. This book outlines how you can use AI to build your brand and generate value for your organization. But this will also mean investment of time and resource on your part, to identify the right tools from the suite I lay out for you, understand them in detail, adapt them to suit your unique needs, use and improvise on them to make it work for you. Remember, there is no silver bullet that will do all of it for you at one stroke. You will need to work and invest on this process, harder than ever. It's a competitive advantage that can be used at this point in time. But the field is ever evolving and you will need to rise to the occasion and keep updating yourself if you want to stay ahead of the curve.

Lastly, there are no guarantees. Nothing is a sure shot recipe for success. All things listed out in this book are the building blocks, tools and techniques to create and build brands. If you work on it diligently, they will help set you on the right path. However, no plan is fool-proof and there are many variables in business that could adversely affect the best-laid plans.

Having said that, success is an outcome of a brilliant strategy and relentless execution, so be positive. Following recommendations and adhering to suggestions should definitely help you change the rules of the game.

Let's explore some of the progress being made in the world of AI to understand how it works and what this unique technology does.

Radiology is an extremely sought-after career in health care and radiologists are among the best-paid medical practitioners. That's because, radiologists are trained to identify anomalies in X-rays, MRI and other critical reports. It's purely their skill that helps doctors make the right diagnosis and prescribe the right treatment to their patients. It takes decades for radiologists to build their expertise, which often is the difference between life and death.

However much has changed in this field over the past few years.

This stream of medical science, with an aura of being the critical factor in identifying illnesses correctly and ensuring that the right treatment is prescribed to patients, now has an alternative to human skill. The field of radiology, considered to be a celebration of unique human intelligence, skill and expertise, is today no longer dependent on human abilities alone.

Impossible as it may sound, it's true.

What's making that happen?

Artificial Intelligence.

How did that happen? To understand this in detail, let us delve into a simplistic explanation of how a radiologist diagnoses a case.

When provided with the case reports, a radiologist studies them to make note of the parts that show deviation from the one of a healthy human. The radiologist then performs a closer inspection cross referencing it with her or his learning, experience and past records and then matches the anomaly with a condition.

When AI systems began working on radiology, they were simply fed tons and tons of existing reports and diagnosis. The system began learning and understanding not just the major aspects, but through machine learning, the finer nuances and differences in conditions as well. It kept improving and reading till it had learnt every aspect of the process. Now it could give the right diagnosis of a condition in a matter of minutes. The medical world then realized another astonishing advantage of the AI system. The AI system was never fatigued irrespective of the number of reports it read. This was a huge benefit. Fatigue is a factor that could affect the functioning of even the best doctors. But the AI system remained fresh throughout the day, 365 days of the year.

Moreover, the AI system showed low errors. Because the AI system relied solely on millions of records for its diagnosis, reducing the probability of errors. All these factors worked to the advantage of AI and today it is an integral part of medical research.

When AI first emerged as a concept, work on it took a broad approach, it tended to look at AI holistically with the perspective that it would affect every aspect of our life and society in a uniform manner. Little bits of progress continued to happen in different spheres, mainly military, research, business and so on. Reports of the progress in the world of AI reached public domain over time and began to be speculated upon in articles lapped up by the average public.

Some of these concepts were picked up by sci-fi writers, film directors and artists who used them as the base to develop their flights of fantasy. Some of the efforts became stunning stories in the form of books and movies that took these concepts into an altogether different realm of possibilities. The sheer magnificence of their creativity caught the fancy of the common public who began to believe that AI could do anything and would alter the future dramatically.

While we have no way of predicting the future, especially the role AI would play in it, what we definitely know is that this broad approach to AI couldn't sustain itself on grandiose concepts and ideas. Frankly, there was just too much speculation with little clarity about its benefits and so, after a few initial sparks, this broad approach to AI finally fizzled out.

Today's boom in AI is driven by its narrow focus. In this approach, rather than look at the entire scope of life and try to initiate small meaningless changes in as many areas as possible, the focus has been to put all effort in fewer narrow portions, where the role of AI can be measured. In these areas the role of AI is significant and makes a real and critical impact in improving the efficiencies of operations. These include medical science, research, communications and intelligence gathering, among others. Soon the role of AI in these industries began to grow so rapidly that the industry players began adopting an AI-first approach to their business.

Sundar Pichai, CEO of Alphabet, Google's parent company stated this intention clearly in 2016 when he said, "It is clear to me we are evolving from a mobile-first to an AI-first world." Shortly after that, Alphabet rolled out two funds, Gradient Ventures and the Google Assistant Investment Program, focused solely on helping Google take a lead over others in the field of AI.

Google isn't the only company using and investing heavily in AI. Alibaba, Apple, Microsoft, IBM, Facebook, Tencent and many other pioneering companies have adopted the AI-first model and have leapfrogged ahead of the curve in their ability to understand and predict consumer behavior using it. AI-based predictive models enable them in providing their customers with unique products and services personalized to their needs. But other companies are not sitting tight either. Every business is getting a sense of the possibilities of using AI in their field and have begun investing in people, data and technology to benefit from the advantages of AI.

Today the size of the AI industry is close to $56 billion and is expected to grow at an average Compound Annual Growth Rate (CAGR) of 40 percent to reach approximately $600 billion by 2027. The figures by themselves mean little, they are merely an indication that this money will get converted into various business applications across different product categories that together will impact our lives significantly. Perhaps, all that sci-fi talk that we were so disdainful about might actually turn into reality earlier than expected!

At the crux of a good AI system is data. The more the data, the more robust will be the resulting AI model. Data has two components to it. The first is the quality of data. Data must be clean and not contain incorrect information. AI follows that golden rule: Garbage In Garbage Out. Contaminated data is the bane of a good system, therefore sufficient effort must be taken to ensure that the data is reviewed, cleaned and authenticated before it becomes the source. Data must be reviewed periodically, because today data being collated on a daily basis is huge, a constant influx of data streams through the system from multiple sources. If adequate checks and measures are not taken, it's highly likely that corrupted data may enter this stream from any of the multiple sources, contaminating the database rapidly and permanently, causing chaos and untold loss.

The second important characteristic of data is its richness. Data being provided must cover a wide swathe of information areas and must have depth. If data is unidimensional, the AI will learn only from the limited resource available in the data pool, making narrow assumptions, leading to mistakes that could do great harm to a company's image. For example, Apple's AI that powered their facial recognition function couldn't detect differences between people in China, which meant that anyone could unlock any iPhone. Microsoft's AI-based chatbot Tay, developed for Twitter conversations with millennials, displayed a racial streak and had to be taken down within 24 hours. Historic data created a bias in Amazon's recruitment AI that tended to have a gender bias favoring men, while IBM's Watson made erroneous recommendations for the treatment of cancer.

While some of it may sound funny and others downright scary, we cannot in all honesty blame the AI for these mistakes. The system only learns from the input and the environment it is provided with. Which is why it is extremely important to first make sure the company has access to significant, clean data, rich in its diversity.

There are two kinds of learning a machine uses to teach itself: Supervised learning and Unsupervised learning.

Supervised learning is when we provide a system with defined data and labels for each set of data and then the system classifies the data basis of the defined parameters into the respective labels. For example, a sports outlet could categorize their inventory according to equipment such as rackets, bats, nets or according to type of sport such as track and field, indoor, aqua, beach, motorized and so on. When this description or input and classification is provided to the system, it will know how to identify fresh inventory and classify them automatically without errors. This is called supervised learning.

In unsupervised learning, there is no input or classification parameter provided to the AI system. So, when it is faced with a task, it will study the data and create classifications for itself. Take the example of the same sports store. If the inventory is provided to an unsupervised system, it will study and classify it by a parameter that may not be regular to the category or understood by humans. For example, this system may classify the equipment according to the material they are made of or their size or their shape.

Both kinds of learning systems have their own advantages and should be applied based on the task at hand.

An unsupervised system is ideal when you want to get fresh ideas from your data, because you are now using the AI to identify patterns that were invisible to the human mind. Take customer segmentation. Most managers and teams live and breathe their customers; sometimes this works to the detriment of an organization as the team is unable to look beyond who they're currently serving, often stymying growth prospects of the brand. An unsupervised system can prove to be of great help here as it could segment the customers according to parameters never considered earlier and throw up interesting targeting opportunities that could provide a fillip to the organization's growth efforts.

It is very important to understand at this juncture exactly how AI works. While I have defined AI as having the ability to behave and offer solutions *like* a human being, it is important to understand the emphasis I have placed on the word *like*. This is critical because most people tend to confuse the word *like* with the word *identical*, which it is not.

AI does not think identical to a human mind. In fact, its method of thinking is very different. Currently, we have little idea about the manner in which machines arrive at their conclusions. Their process is so different that you could very well call it *extraterrestrial*. Researchers and data scientists observing AI systems continuously have come to realize that it is in no way the same as how humans think. Humans learn by observation and behavior, but AI systems learn using associations. These two are very different methods of learning.

When you show an image to an AI system, or play it an audio track or provide it with a book, the machine learns through associations. It builds associations from this input with past data and arrives at different conclusions. This is very different from how a human mind works. AI isn't placing emphasis on the same things that we humans do.

This is both interesting as well as important to bear in mind, as we progress in using this technology for our advancement.

Chapter Summary

1. Ambitious entrepreneurs now have the ability to create brand value by using AI systems to challenge traditional brand-building methods.

2. AI in brand building should not be seen as a cheaper, low-effort alternative to traditional methods. It is simply a smarter opportunity that is relevant to the current times and can become a competitive advantage for brand owners if used well.

3. The rise in computing power has democratized technology, spreading the applications of AI among consumers.

4. AI is different from other programs because it understands the context in which a phrase is written, spoken or seen.

5. The ability of the system to behave and offer solutions *like* a human being is called Artificial Intelligence.

6. The ability of this system to learn from behavior, usage of words, context, tone and reactions is Machine Learning.

7. AI finds many applications in narrow industries where it has made a substantial difference. As more industries adopt AI, it's sphere of influence will spread to impact more and more aspects of our lives in the near future.

8. There are two kinds of learning: Supervised and Unsupervised.

9. AI is dependent on the richness and quality of the data that is fed to it.

10. AI is not without its issues; we need to understand that AI learns by association and its ways of thinking and arriving at conclusions is very different from the ways of the human mind.

CHAPTER 4

Overview

The earlier chapters presented how building a strong brand strategy enhances business value and how by using AI, brands can explore newer routes for creating value. While they enumerated the growing popularity of AI, this chapter throws in a word of caution to ensure that the power of AI is not misconstrued.

- When, where and under what circumstances will AI not be effective.
- What to be cautious about when using AI.
- AI and artificial neural networks.
- Illustrative examples.
- How AI enhances human productivity.
- Difference between AI and software programs of the past.
- How companies perceive AI.
- AI adoption plans in companies.
- The culture barrier to adoption of AI.
- How AI helped in the pandemic.
- AI and the ethical dilemma.

The Caveats of Using AI

Facebook recently made an important admission. For a long period of time, Facebook had believed that it could use AI-based algorithms to identify, control and stop the spread of misinformation, toxic posts and malicious content that sparked negative sentiments on the social networking site. After years of trying with the best technology that this giant has at its disposal, it acknowledged that AI-based algorithms had failed to do the job. Under pressure from lawmakers, Facebook has now changed track. It is now replacing the algorithm with a force of more than ten thousand human evaluators who will scour the site and remove any semblance of hate content. This comes at a time when the world believes in the imminent takeover of human activity by AI. It is a critical piece of information that is important to make us pause and reflect at this juncture that AI too has its flaws and weaknesses. Just like any other tool, to get the best out of it, we must first know what it can do, what its limitations are and how best to utilize its ability.

In the previous chapter we got an introduction to the world of AI, how it was conceived, the trials and errors in its initial journey, how external factors provided it with an impetus and finally how it found its groove and began expanding rapidly. We also covered some definitions, understood the two types of learning and got an overview of how AI processes things. We also explored and understood its benefits when used correctly and got a glimpse of its applications.

While this book will explore the use of AI in brand value creation, as business managers or entrepreneurs, you would also be examining opportunities of using AI for other areas of your business or enterprise. Indeed, it is an exciting area and you must definitely explore every possibility of applying this unique technology to your business. However, just as this area is exciting and filled with opportunities, please bear in mind a few caveats:

AI Cannot Be Used in All Situations

The growth of AI has been spectacular. But on closer inspection, it becomes clear that AI works effectively in some industries, some applications and some areas. This is what we explored when we discussed the narrow focus of AI. Some industries such as online marketing, health care and geo-graphic information systems (GIS) among others find considerable usage and application of AI. These industries have been virtually transformed in a matter of few years. That is because these industries and applications share common characteristic that make the use of AI effective. The characteristics are: Availability of diverse, detailed and excellent sets of data. Data that is continuously improved and updated. Most importantly, the need to take quick actions based on this information. These use cases indicate that AI is ideal for making *Intelligence-based decisions.*

It is also important to evaluate who in the organization is going to be using this information and to what end. Very often, all information in an organization is not critical and is not being used by key decision makers for taking calls that will directly impact the company bottom line. Therefore, one must be judicious and selective when deciding the use of AI. Setting up an AI system, organizing data, testing and implementing it is an expensive and time-consuming process. The end result should be worth the effort. Implementing an AI program for noncritical tasks performed by junior team members won't really create much of an impact for the organization—that's like using a sniper rife to pluck mangoes from a tree. Therefore, ensuring that an AI project delivers *Critical Executive Information*, enabling C-suite executives take decisions to improve the company's performance, is an important reason to implement AI.

AI Is Not a Panacea for Your Business Problems

The worst thing to happen to AI is that it becomes the next fad. AI is not a management jargon to be bragged about. It is meant to improve the intelligence quotient of your organization; help you sift through and analyze humongous data to deliver significant results for your organization. Before you implement an AI project, be clear about its role and the problem or opportunity area you are going to tackle with it. There are many things AI cannot do for sure and it begins with the company vision, strategy and plans. Sometimes businesses adopt expensive practices not fully understanding what it entails. They simply want to create an aura that a lot of effort is being taken, by adopting a practice that's hot and expensive. But such diversions are not going to solve core issues, are they? Fundamental business problems require human intervention in building strategies and implementing rigorous plans to solve them uniquely. These tasks are way beyond what AI can do today. For example, fast food and sodas are increasingly being perceived as unhealthy food by consumers. Similarly, petroleum-based products are also viewed as being harmful to the environment. As these categories start declining, the introduction of AI systems may help improve efficiencies temporarily, but it cannot reverse a negative consumer sentiment. Companies with fundamental financial and business issues need to face up to those challenges and resolve them using relevant strategies and processes. AI can always play a support role by providing robust information, but it cannot solve the underlying issues by itself.

As I have said before, AI is a tool, albeit a very powerful tool. But this tool, like any other is most effective when used for the right task in the right situation. If used incorrectly, it will yield nothing. There's no point in blaming AI or stating that it didn't work, in such circumstances.

You May Not Need AI

This could also be a reality that must be explored. Not all weapons in the armory need to be deployed in battle. Sometimes simpler tools used smartly can be more effective. You must not implement AI in a field or department or vertical, simply because you have the resource at your disposal. Or because AI worked well for you elsewhere. It is important to understand the task at hand and evaluate the use of existing tools to solve it. Chances are, they will.

If in doubt, always evaluate the application of AI by performing a Return-on-Investment (ROI) analysis. It may involve some thinking, evaluation, information and time, but it's the best metrics to understand if the effort and resource that's going to be invested in building an AI project for the task, is going to be worth it. You will have a clear and definite answer at the end of the analysis and you can then progress in whichever direction, with confidence and assurance.

Be Educated and Careful When Using AI

AI is fast becoming a buzzword. This is attracting a lot of positive as well as negative elements to it. Like every category that's nascent, a lot of what is passed around is hearsay and may not be rooted in truth. In the hurry to adopt the most modern practices, ensure that you do not get lured by the promises of fly-by-night operators making dubious claims. From incorrect advice on what AI can do, to improper installation, blemished data and setting grandiose expectations, be prepared to be flooded by hordes of companies hawking false, fake and misleading products and services. Beware of buying data without verifying its details. Remember, as data regulations become stringent and enforced by governments world-wide, you could be exposing your organization to risk.

Modern AI is founded on an established idea of artificial neural networks. In this technique, an artificial network mimics the way the human brain learns. So, when training data is passed through an artificial network, the network fine-tunes to the incoming data and uses this information to predict future data.

This gives us a good perspective to understand where and how AI applications could be of particular service. A good AI system has the ability to read vast amounts of data, find patterns and take predefined actions based on the patterns that emerge from the data. In short, it is of particular use in areas where there is a lot of different sets of input data to be studied, various outcomes to be analyzed and different actions to be taken in each case. This kind of a situation would normally take humans a lot of effort and analysis. It would also need many levels of iterations, checks and approvals, all of which would lock up a lot of resources in terms of talent, cost and time.

Take for example weather predictions. It's a thankless task that's received more than its fair share of ridicule. Weather forecasters are regularly made fun of by comedians, cartoonists and even by regular people when initiating small talk. And they are not entirely wrong because weather prediction is truly a challenging task. In the past weather prediction had to rely on a wide range of sources collating and deciphering, which is a herculean task. To make matters more difficult, atmospheric conditions tend to change rapidly, multiplying data, increasing the complexity for the analysts and forecasters. Missing one tiny factor, leads to a completely erroneous forecast that gets savagely trolled across media. However, today AI can help perform the same task more efficiently and predict the weather correctly with a high degree of accuracy in many cases.

In fact, one of China's television networks uses an AI-powered reporter to present the weather forecasts in a popular regional channel.

This is possible because AI is able to sift through tons of data, adopt the right analysis models, compare data with other inputs, track and follow patterns that were hitherto ignored or missed and above all, develop its own algorithm to generate predictions that are not just general but specific for different audiences such as city dwellers, maritime traders, farmers, fishermen and so on. The benefit of this information is significant for people in the above trade. By predicting weather patterns and seasonality trends, AI can aid farmers in their practices. It can connect possible crops with predicted prices in the markets and advice farmers on what produce will yield maximum return. This information not just improves the ROI of the farmer, but also reduces his workload and efforts considerably.

In sum, AI is taking away the burden of strenuous and repetitive work that sucks up our time. This is the real advantage of AI. All of us enjoy that part of our work, which is stimulating, exciting and helps us discover new things. What makes work dull and uninviting is the amount of grunt work that simply needs to be done every day to get to the interesting part. Unfortunately, this repetitive grunt work is what takes up 70 percent of our working time, leaving us exhausted to do the really exciting stuff. With the rise of AI, we can expect the rapid reduction of these repetitive tasks, freeing us to perform to our optimum capabilities. This is the biggest benefit of AI for mankind. It is the reason why, despite all the misinformation surrounding it, AI will continue to grow and impact our lives.

AI is different from other software programs of the past. Earlier software programs were information keyed into a system by a human and the program merely followed that coded instruction set. AI is different because it doesn't work within the boundaries of a preprogrammed set of rules. It actually begins to create and improvise the rules as it learns. AI is iterative and improves continuously. The rise of AI will inevitably impact our lives and our work and the way we do things. As the technology finds newer applications in varied industries, traditional methods relevant till now, will begin fading away.

For the better.

Industries will become more efficient, more data-driven, more productive. The roles of people working in those organizations will also change. Traditional organization structure, in which the thinking happens only at the top and execution is done by the layers below will begin to change and flatten. The requirements and resultant information connected with AI will affect not merely the structure but also the skills and roles within functions. High-quality information will reduce the need for judgment-based decision making, impacting leadership profile and structure.

Will experience be a boon or a bane? On one hand, an employee's decades of experience is worth its weight in gold. But all this could change in an environment where AI systems render experience inconsequential. AI systems will not only bring in varied and rich data but will also provide dynamic solutions making experience meaningless.

On the other hand, freshers with a good hang of the subject, could perhaps give nascent technologies shape and create new and powerful augmented systems from them. Therefore, not only could there be an implosion of the current organization structures, there might even be a reordering of the structure, where talent and knowledge in AI could carry more weight than the experience of an older, outdated world.

This is a wakeup call for all of us. There is bound to be an environmental change. Our current skills will be questioned and tested and the value we bring to our roles will be scrutinized, perhaps by a machine someday. There will be no place to hide, no worth for paper-pushers and no boundaries for those willing to adapt and grow.

The best way forward for working professionals is to prepare themselves for the inevitable change. Begin by understanding the context of AI in your industry and the areas that it could impact. The next important requirement is to keep an open mind. Set aside time to read up on the subject especially relevant to your industry. Attend AI seminars, webinars, workshops and meet people in affiliated industries. Begin to develop a concept for application of AI in your industry and offer to spearhead a small project within your organization. If you do this much with sincerity, I can assure you that you will be a changed person in the matter of a few months. Whether the project takes off or not, you will!

AI is being gradually adopted by more and more companies. According to a 2019 Harvard Business Review article, *Building the AI-Powered Organization* by Tim Fountaine, Brian McCarthy and Tamim Saleh, of the companies they surveyed, only 8 percent have deployed AI in core practices that will impact the entire organization. The other organizations seem to be circumspect of AI, treating it as a test case restricted to a limited field. The biggest barrier according to the article is the organization's culture and an inertia to change.

AI is always going to face this challenge in adoption. Large traditional companies believe that success is their automatic right and is an outcome of their culture and current practices. They treat AI as important but prefer to adopt a "wait and watch attitude." To hedge their bets, they may initiate small projects, with the belief that doing this should be good enough to judge the potency of the tool. Unfortunately, this could be counterproductive. A half-hearted approach in AI will prove to be of little benefit, supporting the belief that AI is not relevant to an organization. Successful implementation of AI requires top management to be all-in. To reap its benefits, one must have an AI-first approach to the business. This necessitates investment from the entire organization.

The HBR article goes on to specify,

> AI has the biggest impact when it's developed by cross-functional teams with a mix of skills and perspectives. Having business and operational people work side by side with analytics experts will ensure that initiatives address broad organizational priorities, not just isolated business issues. Diverse teams can also think through the operational changes new applications may require—they're likelier to recognize, say, that the introduction of an algorithm that predicts maintenance needs should be accompanied by an overhaul of maintenance workflows. And when development teams involve end users in the design of applications, the chances of adoption increase dramatically.

Sometimes, an external stimulus, even a negative one can spur quick adoption. The recent COVID pandemic has highlighted the importance of adopting AI. According to a report by MIT Technology Review Insights in association with Arm, in their November 30, 2020, article titled, "A new horizon: Expanding the AI landscape":

In a recent MIT Technology Review Insights survey of 301 business and technology leaders, 38% report their AI investment plans are unchanged as a result of the pandemic, and 32% indicate the crisis has accelerated their plans. The percentages of unchanged and revved up AI plans are greater at organizations that had an AI strategy already in place.

Consumers and business decision-makers are realizing that there are many ways that AI augments human effort and experience. Technology leaders in most organizations regard AI as a critical capability that has accelerated efforts to increase operational efficiency, gain deeper insight about customers, and shape new areas of business innovation.

The purpose of sharing this information is to allow you to take some time out and think about the increasing role that AI will play in our work and personal lives in the future. Hopefully, it will trigger a chain of thought leading to actions that make AI an integral part of your function, organization and role. At a personal level, you should be considering the areas of AI that you can relate with, to explore, learn and build expertise in.

Vietnam's use of AI in the early days of the COVID pandemic proved to be extremely useful in preventing cases from rising rapidly, unlike the rest of the world. This was achieved by using a mix of facial recognition technology, chatbots, predictive mapping, disseminating the right education on social media platforms and having doctors available on telephone calls. Using facial recognition, an infected individual's journey was mapped and the people the carrier was in touch with were contacted, tested and quarantined. A unique web-based application allowed individuals to log in and check their past journeys to know if they had been in a COVID hotspot. Then using predictive techniques, Vietnam could foretell the next COVID cluster by analyzing a variety of seemingly unrelated parameters such as weather, population density in key areas and search trends. This enabled them to set up a warning system that informed citizens beforehand, thereby reducing the chance of infections. By pairing news articles with COVID maps, Vietnam successfully identified spots of misinformation and prevented the spread of rumors. Another interesting aspect was their use of doctors on video conferencing facility to help diagnose patients with COVID-like symptoms.

Going forward, AI could help us improve our product and service experience in a number of industry verticals. But along with the good that AI can do, there's also the rise of the negative use of AI especially in Deepfakes. Deepfakes are basically using AI to impersonate a human by creating images and videos that are fake. There's a lot of positive that can be achieved by this technology. Take, for example, David Beckham's ad on behalf of the NGO, Malaria Must Die. Synthesia AI used Deepfake technology to make David Beckham speak in nine different languages. Beckham's global popularity combined with the technology that enabled him to speak and sound natural in many local languages, helped immensely in spreading the important message successfully in many countries. This technology is finding immense applications be it in fashion, providing life-like trial simulations in apparel retail, or bringing yesteryear stars of the silver screen alive on digital platforms, as well as localizing communication as evident from the David Beckham example.

Unfortunately, the good is often accompanied by the bad. Deepfakes can be misused in cybercrimes, pornography and also exposes companies to cyberattacks through voice-matching techniques. Unfortunately, the negative news always gets undue coverage in media due to their sensational nature and overshadow the improvements that AI brings about. As professionals, we must be pragmatic and accept the reality that any technology will always have its fair share of criticism. In fact, that should only spur further development in ensuring safer standards. In summation, we need to consider any technology from its holistic perspective rather than get bogged down by the occasional negative news that it will inevitably attract. The focus of our energy should be in refining the technology, improving the experience for our customers and society at large.

As the field of AI becomes more significant and as its influence in our society and lifestyle becomes more prevalent, there are bound to be many more areas of friction and questions that will arise. While this book is restricted to providing practical applications of AI in brand building, it is important to make the reader aware of some of the ethical dilemmas concerning AI that are widespread and are currently under consideration and discussion.

The Thought Process of Machines Is a Mystery

While AI and machine learning can help us categorize and cluster data efficiently and uniquely, the machine cannot tell us the *reason* why it categorized or clustered data in that manner. This remains a dark area for researchers and users of AI. Therefore, trusting the AI to make independent decisions is not possible. There have been instances of loans being denied to people of a certain background, based purely on their racial profiling. This caused a huge embarrassment for the company involved.

Permission Issues

Today AI systems capture our personal and professional data from a number of sources. Right from the moment we land at the airport of a city, facial recognition devices and even our cell phone data starts recording our journeys. When we search online, visit social media sites and make comments, we leave behind a trail of data that's gobbled up and analyzed by AI. While a lot of this is done to help provide us with better targeted products, the fact remains that this information is being collected sometimes without our knowledge.

Increased Threat and Exposure to Fraudsters

Deepfakes have raised questions about impersonations and misuse. In the wrong hands, this technology can be used to create fake videos and images that incite viewers on social media sites, stroking violent reactions. Similarly, fraudsters can impersonate known people and commit serious economic crimes.

Threat to Jobs

Perhaps the biggest concerns that people have is that AI will take away our jobs leading to huge economic and social upheaval.

There are no easy and ready answers to these dilemmas. The discussions and debates on these topics will continue to happen and cannot be concluded in haste. We need to come to terms with the reality that we may have to give up some things we considered precious, in order to gain bigger things. Then it becomes a matter of defining boundaries for both.

Hopefully reason and good sense will prevail and humanity will be able to come up with a system that puts adequate checks and balances in place, ensuring that scientific progress does not come at the cost of important human values.

Chapter Summary

1. There are some caveats to keep in mind about AI:
   1.1. AI cannot be used in all situations.
   1.2. AI is not a panacea for your business problems.
   1.3. You may not need AI.
   1.4. Be educated and careful when you use AI.
2. AI is based on the concept of artificial neural networks that mimics the way the human mind works.
3. AI is of particular use in areas that are data rich and complex.
4. AI takes away the grunt work allowing humans to focus on quality tasks.
5. AI doesn't work within the boundaries of a preprogrammed set of rules. It actually begins to create and improvise the rules as it learns. AI is an iterative process that continuously improves by itself.
6. AI is bound to impact a number of industries and shake the way they are currently structured.
7. Working professionals should embrace AI and lead the change in their respective organizations.
8. The biggest roadblock to adopting AI is corporate inertia and culture. This must change for companies to benefit from the opportunity that AI provides.
9. There are a number of ethical dilemmas about the use of AI that need to be resolved.
10. The use of AI to fight the COVID pandemic provides us with an insight of the greater good that AI delivers.

CHAPTER 5

Overview

The previous chapters provided a broad overview of AI, some key definitions, caveats and why AI will play an important role in the future. This chapter will begin our journey into understanding how AI can help in brand building.

- The importance of consumer insight in business.
- Building an AI system.
- Availability of rich consumer data online.
- Access to consumer data on large internet company platforms.
- AI tools to understand different aspects of consumer behavior.
- Getting a granular understanding of your market, customer and future trends using AI.
- How AI enables a richer retail experience.

Using AI to Identify and Get Insights About Customers

People tend to put on a façade when they post their profiles on dating apps. With posturing and grandstanding becoming the order of the day, the focus on these sites swung toward accumulating "swipe rights." With the category attracting newer players regularly, this behavior soon became the norm with everyone intent on presenting a perfect picture of themselves and choosing to hide their vulnerabilities. Departing from this norm, the dating app Hinge used AI to identify consumer insights and soon found that an extremely high number—over 80 percent—of their user base hadn't managed to find a long-term relationship on any swiping app, ever. A bitter truth that no user on the app would openly admit to. Based on this insight, Hinge developed a remarkable campaign titled "Let's be real," and encouraged users to share their vulnerabilities on the app to find a better, long-term match for themselves. This connected deeply with the true desires of consumers and resulted in a 4x increase in Hinge's user base. This highlights how AI-driven consumer insights can be a game changer for brands enabling them to improvise on their product delivery and design relevant communication to touch the right chords in the consumers' hearts.

I trust that at the end of the previous chapter your interest in the possibilities of AI has turned from a general sense of curiosity into excitement at the likelihood of finding applications for it in your enterprise, work or field of study. Hopefully, your mind is whirring with ideas on how you could put AI to use and tackle challenging issues that have been eating up endless amounts of your time, frustrating you and your colleagues and preventing you from rising above mundane issues to apply your mind to larger strategic matters that you are experienced, trained and qualified to do.

Indeed, it is a shame that so many professionals spend considerable amount of their valuable time in tackling the same set of issues on a daily basis, repeatedly, throughout their careers. There is of course, a downside to this. First, it is a waste of talent. Professionals are skilled, trained and capable of solving diverse sets of issues, be it opportunities or problems. While we may seem daunted initially by seemingly gargantuan tasks, most professional teams inevitably rise to such challenges and find a suitable method or solution, to solve the challenge.

Many organizations have developed processes and techniques to tackle opportunities and challenges, as they emerge. Management literature is replete with stellar examples of organizations and teams using time-tested or out-of-the-box processes to solve matters and grow their organizations rapidly. At other times, teams break out of the stifling and rigid shackles of processes and use common sense to come up with clutter-breaking ideas that are the solution for their growth. In India, we have a term for this. We call it *Jugaad*. To understand what jugaad is, let's first understand what an organization problem is!

An organization problem, in simple language, is the occurrence of a situation that is unexpected and that has the potential to disrupt the smooth functioning of operations. Sometimes it is compounded by the realization that the organization is ill-equipped or lacks adequate information to solve it. In a typical professional environment, when a problem occurs, the process assigned to handle problems simply takes over. All professional organizations usually have Standard Operating Procedures (SOPs) in place to handle such issues. However, when problems go beyond the realm of past experience and established processes, that is when human creativity, resourcefulness and teamwork comes into play. Solution themes that follow an acceptable path are called procedures or techniques, if problem-solving methods are put in play. But in some cases, solutions require more than process and technique to solve problems. In such circumstances, new theories are invented and tested before being put into production. This is product or process innovation leading to *the creation of something new and never created before.*

Jugaad is innovation too, but of a different kind. It is the ability to solve problems by creatively piecing together a workable solution with whatever components are readily available at hand. If you search the web for the term *jugaad* you will find a number of examples of common Indians using jugaad in everyday life. From using a trouser to split the air of an air cooler to cool two rooms simultaneously, to running a water pump using a motorcycle, the cases of jugaad are both inspiring as well as entertaining. But there are many genuine cases of entrepreneurs using jugaad to solve practical problems and create thriving businesses.

For example, a company called Husk Powered Systems today provides power to over 25,000 homes in India by creating energy from discarded rice husk. This not just empowers thousands of rural families but is also an environmentally friendly method of power generation.

The point I'm trying to make through this is that humans and professionals thrive when faced with opportunities and problems because that is when they're at their creative best. The most stymieing experience for professional managers is having to do the same job over and over again, repeatedly. This not only sucks away the spark of enthusiasm and creativity from managers and entrepreneurs, but after a certain point, it dulls them into a sense of nonchalance. The most harmful effect of such work is to reduce the once sharp and enterprising professionals into unimaginative cookie cutters.

AI can take away the dulling repetitive tasks allowing managers and entrepreneurs the freedom to tackle real-world issues. Implementation of AI should only help spur improvement and forge professionals into competent and enterprising managers buzzing with ideas and innovation!

While the possibilities of AI sound exciting, the pragmatic reader could be keen to know how they could implement AI in their organizations.

There are two ways you can implement AI within your organization. The first is to build your own AI system. This begins with identifying an appropriate area or function within your organization. If you recall, the key tenet for creating a successful AI project is data. Select a field or function that has access to diverse quality data. You then need to define your problem or opportunity statement that the AI will solve and set your objectives accordingly. On completing this step, resource and talent requirements will become evident. First put together a cross-functional team qualified to perform the task. Next provide the required resources to achieve the objectives. Finally set goals and timelines that are achievable. Monitor regularly and course correct depending on progress.

This is the starting point for you to build a future-focused AI-driven organization.

But what if you lack the resources?

The other option is to use ready-to-use readily available online AI tools and apply it to your problem or opportunity statement.

Our objective is to use AI for brand value creation, hence let me explain to you how AI applications can be used in your brand-building efforts.

To begin with, the core of any brand is the customer. Without the customer, there is no need and so there is no brand. One of the fundamental reasons why brands fail is because they fail to identify their customers correctly. Their customer segmentation is either too broad or too narrow or in some cases, not defined at all.

Don't be surprised to hear this. In my career, I have often been greeted with blank stares to my question, "Who is your customer?" Brands and organizations are so caught up with their product that they fail to understand that the product is only relevant if it solves a consumer need, irrespective of how beautiful, multifeatured or futuristic it may look, sound or behave. Of what relevance is a product, if all it evokes is a round of applause but leaves the cash register silent?

On further probing, by asking for a definition of the individual who could require such a product, I have been often told, "Oh! Anybody is my customer because everyone needs this product."

This answer is reminiscent of the Calvin and Hobbes cartoon strip, in which Calvin's stall provides "A swift kick in the butt" for a dollar. Unsurprisingly, there aren't any takers, but when Hobbes wonders why, Calvin replies, "I don't understand. Everyone I know needs it!"

Business history is replete with such instances. In India, a successful consumer durable company spent huge money to launch the world's first "vacuumizer." According to the company, Indians had a habit of stocking up on snacking items called *farsan*. These were like crisps and fritters that are a staple accompaniment served with tea in India. Indians being a thrifty lot, prefer buying these snacks or making them at home, in large quantities to lower costs.

With time, these snacks tend to lose their crispness, flavor and taste in storage, which is a cause for dissatisfaction among customers. This loss of crispness was attributed to the presence of air in the containers that stored the farsan. Believing that they had struck on a very important insight, the company invested all their resources in developing and engineering a unique product, "the vacuumizer." The product "vacuumizer" was a set of plastic containers that came along with a vacuum pump. The farsan bought in bulk could be stored in these containers, which would then be rendered "air-free" through the use of the vacuumizer pump that would remove all air in the closed containers. Each time a housewife opened the container to remove farsan, all she had to do was to shut the container and use the pump to eject out the trapped air. In this manner, the company argued, precious farsan would remain fresh for weeks together.

The media launch was no less spectacular. The company bought a media blackout all over the country on the day of their launch, a remarkable feat in terms of media innovation at the time. They took advertising spots on all the major television channels at the same time slot to launch this unique concept. This was followed through with a barrage of communication, cutting across every type of media vehicle. Unfortunately, despite their best efforts, the housewife was unimpressed by the vacuumizer. The product sank like a cement block, taking the company with it.

The company was so much in awe of their product, that they had believed "Every home needed it!" The reality was that while housewives regretted having to serve stale farsan, they saw no point in paying a huge sum—the equivalent of a television set—for a device that kept farsan fresh. The pragmatic housewives, saw better value in making or buying less quantity of farsan periodically than having to invest in an expensive machine only to pump air out of it every day.

So, knowing your customer well and identifying the right insight, is pivotal to your brand strategy.

Today, a lot of purchase and evaluation happens online. Customers search, compare, evaluate, read up on products and then check out available offers before making a purchase.

Convenience rules the world now. The earlier view that customers need to touch, feel and experience a product before purchase is now passe. Consumers happily buy expensive mobiles, laptops, televisions and even cars online. Even categories once considered personal, such as clothes, lingerie and jewelry are being purchased online. The COVID pandemic has only strengthened this trend further. During the lockdown as the world began adapting to norms of social distancing and operating from home, online portals and websites often became the lifeline for people in every part of the world, supplying a variety of goods, ranging from everyday essentials to lifestyle elements and consumer durables.

The internet also became the primary source of information and education. Now as the world limps back to normalcy, it remains the preferred destination because people have got used to its convenience, benefitting in more ways than they expected from it, thereby making it a habit.

All this has only fueled the growth and importance of AI. As mentioned earlier, the most critical factor for AI to be effective is the availability of data. The COVID pandemic has proved to be a major catalyst for driving people online. This has led to a boom of consumer activity on the internet with people from all over the world searching for everything from pharmaceutical products to entertainment options online, providing AI tools with a rich lode of data. Companies such as Google, Facebook, Amazon, Microsoft and many other large and small players who are AI driven, have received tremendous inputs, enriching their consumer knowledge and intelligence. This information is being used to create more effective and efficient business and consumer online interactions.

Consumer insights and behavior is the cornerstone of an effective brand-building strategy. Using the information available online, you can get to know your customer better. You can now understand how they begin their search process, what triggers their interests, where do they go to get more information, who are their influencers, what is the topic of conversation with friends and family, how do families decide, what sites do they visit, what's their favorite food, destination, purchase intent for products, outlook to life and society, interests, social causes, entertainment preferences, and so on.

The list is endless, but useful for you to get a clear idea about the different kinds of audiences who show interest in your brand. This information will help you build a diverse execution plan that can be personalized for each target audience. Your website analytics data will tell you how consumers land on your site, how do they behave, what parts of your website is engaging, which parts do not hold their interest, what path the consumers use to purchase the product or service, the factors enabling sales and reasons to drop off.

All of this information is invaluable as you get to understand your customer better and understand their journey in acquiring your brand. This knowledge will enable you to fine-tune your offering and provide them with the right set of information and incentives to acquire your brand with minimum fuss.

These are some of the areas that AI-enabled consumer understanding tools can help you gather information about.

Trend Analysis

AI can help you understand the important consumer trends that are relevant and current. What seems to be the favorite holiday destination the coming summer? Which cuisine appears to be the hot favorite? What kind of clothes will trend? What seems to have caught people's attention in home décor? What are the trending colors in cosmetics? A variety of categories and niches get covered by analyzing the humongous amounts of data and interactions that are happening online. These conversations are captured and from this data, trends can be spotted. The trends are further split and scrutinized to understand the inherent strength of each trend. For some trends could simply be fads that fizzle out after a short burst of interest. The purpose of sifting through all the options is to identify the trend that has the strongest potential and most affinity among consumers. These are the trends that a brand has to correctly identify and build strategies around.

Brands can also determine the potential of different trends and their variations by analyzing the strength of the consumer affinity for them. With this data, brands can plan for future variants taking a lead in their development to surprise their consumer with ideas just at the moment they're taking root among consumers, almost like a coincidence. Tools such as Xineoh, Google Trends and Facebook Audience Insights are some that can be explored in this regard.

Sentiment Analysis

Having identified a trend, you may want to know more about the associations that consumers make with it and the related topics that the consumer could possibly be interested in. This analysis indicates the breadth and scope of a brand's appeal. The wider the appeal the greater are the chances of the brand's interaction with the category. For example, consumers in the market for a new home could be interested in understanding how well the locality is connected or about schooling options in and around the neighborhood. They could also be reading up about the air quality, safety and other aspects connected to living in the area. Now these reasons are rarely factored in the selling strategy of real-estate projects that essentially focus on size of the homes, amenities and facilities. But by understanding the sentiment of the customer, the brand can include these topics in their content strategy, thereby connecting better with potential customers. Often these aspects swing the customer decision in the favor of a brand when everything else is at par with competition.

Identifying the right sentiment demonstrates a deeper understanding of customer needs, which can then be worked into an advantage by providing the customer with the right information and service. Tools such as Chorus are some that can help in creating a richer more involved conversation with potential customers seeking a better interaction with brands. Then you have predictive tools such as Arimo that tracks shopper behavior online and predicts their purchase intent. This information is vital and brands can use it to customize their offering to the right audience at the right time.

Experience Analysis

Your customer is at the center of your brand-building effort. Today marketing and brand-building efforts are moving away from the generic to the specific. While earlier we would have a broad definition of the consumer based on demographic and psychographic parameters, in the digital world of today, we have the ability to get more granular insights into their behavior. Web-based analytical tools can paint an extremely detailed picture of your customer. Deploying and using these tools will enable you to get an exact picture of who your customer is, how your customer is behaving and what is working. Analytics can help you determine the following three key aspects:

Source: Answers all the key questions about what is the effectiveness of your current marketing and messaging campaigns: Where did the consumer reach your website from? Was it on a related site, blog, video? Which ad did the consumer click? What were the performance matrices of your ad network? What message seems to work? Which social media channels are working best for you? What search terms is the consumer using to reach you? Which category of e-mails seem to be generating the maximum impact? This information could be crucial in helping you focus on your future Search Engine Optimization (SEO), content, advertising and marketing strategy.

Profile: This will tell you exactly who your customers are. You can set aside all ambiguity because now you know the profile of the person. Or rather, profiles. Because the granularity of the information will start differentiating people for who they are. Get to know their age, gender, demographic, geography, preferences, tastes and more. Customers begin appearing like real, identifiable people, so you can understand their needs and the role your brand plays in their lives.

Usage: Perhaps the most important because this captures how the consumer interacted on the website. Heat maps and video tracking can provide an exact idea of how the consumer traversed the site, identifying spots they found engaging and where they spent time. Get to know their consideration parameters, triggers for purchase and locate parts where they left your site. The right objectives will help track the customer journey across a predetermined path and understand its effectiveness. Get to know the factors that ensured the achievement of objectives and the factors preventing them.

Beside Google Analytics, tools such as Leadfeeder will help you better your sales conversions. Live site visualization tools will help you better understand what people are looking for in your website.

Chatter Analysis

What are people saying about your brand, where are the conversations headed? Is there important information about your product or service that consumers have failed to pick up? Does your competition have features that consumers find irresistible? Are your customers feeling hurt about something your brand did or said? Where do you feature in your consumers' world?

In the dynamic age we live in, consumer chatter often makes or breaks a brand. In India, a popular jewelry brand ran an advertisement featuring an interfaith marriage. Social media erupted as the ad polarized netizens, some speaking for and others against the ad. The brand pulled out the ad to assuage sentiments but somehow the topic did not fully die out. The online conversations continued increasing in bitterness, with numerous calls to boycott the brand. A few months later, when the brand launched another festival ad, it only rekindled the negative sentiments and many netizens took umbrage to the new ad, pointing out that it contained elements that hurt their cultural sentiments.

This highlights the long tail or persistent effect of content in the online world. The internet has a long memory and brands can no longer claim that they alone control the narrative around their brands. Tools such as NetBase and other text analyzing tools provide brands with the real picture of the conversations surrounding them, enabling them to devise communication that is relevant and connected with the prevalent consumer sentiment.

Interaction Analysis

How did your salesperson's conversation with the customer go? Did your representative at the retail outlet paint the right picture? Are your e-mails effectively conveying the brand message? Did you respond well to customer queries?

In the past, there was no way to know the course of these interactions. There was little or no response mechanisms, limited learning and few avenues of follow through that could be planned. Feedback was what the rep wrote back and the only metrics for a diverse set of efforts was sales. If the sales were good, everything worked, if not, there was no way to identify where the problem lay. Leading to that famous quote by an advertiser, "Half the money I spend on advertising is wasted; Trouble is, I don't know which half."

Today AI has enabled a number of tools to provide brands with the ability to analyze these conversations. From telephone calls, to e-mails to chat messages and social media posts. You now have the ability to learn from all of these conversations. Fact is, the first person to tell you if your brand's promise works or not, is your customer. Now you have the ability to analyze hundreds of thousands of customer conversations and better still, understand the issues or the problems that they are encountering. This information is available instantaneously and you can immediately take corrective action, making a huge difference to business operations.

Products such as Signal AI process thousands of customer conversations. These conversations can be compared with those from the past to identify areas of concern and build relevant solutions.

These are just some examples and a few possibilities that exist today for brands to get consumer insights from. There's no area that can claim to be bereft of ready-to-use AI-enabled tools. For most sectors, there are tools abound to help you understand your customer better, track their behavior, analyze their actions, understand their interactions, follow up with conversations and take corrective action whenever required.

Today, a brand cannot hide behind market research and blame research techniques for failing to provide them with the right insight. Soon, no excuse will be acceptable for lack of information about how consumers interact, what they experience, why they fail to convert and what they're talking about with others, because all of this is available or will soon be available in real time at your fingertips.

A supermarket chain in South Africa found an interesting correlation in their counter sales. Across all stores in the chain, sales of baby diapers seemed to increase proportionally with the sale of beer. Especially in the evenings. At first the company ignored this data, after all sale of baby diapers and milk was an understandable correlation, but baby diapers and beer? Impossible!

However, the persistence of the information raised their curiosity to give the matter a closer look. When they dug deeper, they realized that the sale of both products was indeed connected and why this was happening.

In most homes with a baby, it was usually in the evenings when mothers, checking their baby's inventories for the night would realize that they were short of diapers. This was about the time when the menfolk would be settling down to watch their favorite sport on TV. On realizing the shortage, they would be promptly dispatched to the nearest store to get diapers for the baby. With the anticipation of an exciting match high on their minds, the men would inadvertently pick up a sixpack along with the diapers. An understanding of this behavior ensured that the store packed beer cans close to the diaper section, leading to a significant increase in beer sales.

Insights from AI aren't just restricted to the online world. AI can help you understand how your consumer buys in every environment, including retail. Analysis of purchase data can throw up interesting and significant correlations between diverse sets of products, you never believed were connected. The truth is that our experience sometimes acts like blinkers, preventing us from seeing facts, even when they are laid out bare in front of us.

Most stores are aware of customers who purchased from them. The details of their purchase are available to track and correlate due to their purchase records. But what of the countless shoppers who walked out without purchasing anything? In most shops, a far larger number of people walk out without shopping. No store keeps any record of them or why these customers went out. Their walk into the store is indication of interest. How did they behave once they were in? What was the section that they visited? What products did they browse? How many of them tried on products? Why didn't they buy what they tried on? Did they find the right fit? Color? Design? Were they looking for a bargain? Did they check the online store when they were shopping?

AI-enabled facial tracking can provide brands with answers to these questions by analyzing consumer behavior inside the store. It can collate a wide spectrum of information be it a single store or multilocation chain. It can provide you with correlations, indicate what customers found interesting and where they dropped off. It can highlight interest in fit, color and designs for brands to ingest and use in their next creation. It can also predict how customers will behave in the future and provide insights on smaller matters such as, whether too many changing rooms are good or bad and what small touches could improve the store experience.

Did the celebrity images on the walls make an impact? Are the aisles comfortable to move or do they cause irritation? What can be improved in the checkout stage? How many frustrated customers simply set aside their selection and left? Can customers get instant recommendations inside the store similar to online portals?

There's no end to the kind of change that AI can bring to any kind of business. AI can predict the consumers who will return for purchase and why others won't. This can help brands tailor-make strategies for different sets of customers and begin conversations with them.

Indeed, the pandemic has caused a shift in consumer behavior and purchase habits. But while a lot of this will continue, there's no reason to believe that customers won't return to physical stores or that brick-and-mortar retail is dead. Humans are essentially social creatures and also resilient. Humanity will prevail and humans will learn to adapt to such scenarios in the future. Companies and brands must also learn to adapt to the evolving consumer too. Adapting with changing times is the best way to survive. One only needs to examine the category of tablet phones. People said tablets would kill laptops or phones or desktops, but that didn't happen. All of them continue to coexist and each has found its own niche. Retail will too, as long as you use information to evolve and keep your customer engaged.

Chapter Summary

1. AI replaces repetitive mundane tasks allowing professionals to focus on high-value creative work.

2. Customer is the most critical element of a successful business, therefore understanding customers well is the most important focus for any business.

3. Identifying the right consumer insight and building on it, is often the difference between success and failure.

4. The first step to having an effective AI program is to set the objectives correctly.

5. There are two ways you can implement AI within your organization. The first is to build your own AI system.

6. The second is to use AI-enabled tools that are readily available.

7. The COVID pandemic has caused a significant shift in the customer behavior, with most consumers now showing preference for buying online, providing data and information to helping develop AI-enabled analytics tools for consumer insights.

8. AI-enabled tools provide customer insights and information on: Trend analysis, sentiment analysis, experience analysis, chatter analysis and interaction analysis.

9. AI can also be used to analyze customer data for brick-and-mortar stores providing invaluable insights for strategy development.

10. With the right objectives, the right set of tools and having a disciplined approach, brands can understand consumer behavior with a great degree of granularity enabling the creation of unique engagement strategies.

CHAPTER 6

Overview

The previous chapter throws light on how AI can enable brands to develop a deep understanding of the customer. This chapter builds on it, enabling the development of brand strategy.

- How to use AI to develop effective marketing strategies.
- Developing the right audience clusters.
- Personalizing products and services with AI.
- Structuring a communication channel using AI.
- Using AI to keep a tab on competition.
- AI tools for category analysis.
- Adaptable AI tools for specific business needs.
- The Entrepreneur's AI Tools Suite.
- AI as a personal assistant.
- Legal documentation understanding with AI.
- Human Resource made easy with AI.
- Cyber security using AI.

AI and Brand Development

Harley Davidson in 2016 credited 40 percent of its sales in New York City to Albert. Their dealership in New York, which was selling about one to two vehicles per week zoomed to 15, the week Albert came onboard and kept growing from thereon.

Sounds magical, doesn't it? So, who do you think is Albert?

Albert isn't a Hollywood or sports celebrity. Neither is he a biking enthusiast or champion. Albert isn't the dealership's star salesperson and no, Albert isn't the name of a biker community nor the leader of a cult either.

In fact, Albert is not even a person. Albert is an AI-powered platform.

To give you an idea of how it worked, here's an extract from the article, "How Harley-Davidson Used Artificial Intelligence to Increase New York Sales Leads by 2,930%" by Brad Power that was featured in the Harvard Business Review.

In the case of Harley-Davidson, the AI tool, Albert, drove in-store traffic by generating leads, defined as customers who express interest in speaking to a salesperson by filling out a form on the dealership's website.

Armed with creative content (headlines and visuals) provided by Harley-Davidson, and key performance targets, Albert began by analyzing existing customer data from the outlet's customer relationship management (CRM) system to isolate defining characteristics and behaviors of high-value past customers: those who either had completed a purchase, added an item to an online cart, viewed website content, or were among the top 25 percent in terms of time spent on the website.

Using this information, Albert identified lookalikes who resembled these past customers and created micro segments— small sample groups with whom Albert could run test campaigns before extending its efforts more widely. It used the data gathered through these tests to predict which possible headlines and visual combinations—and thousands of other campaign variables— would most likely convert different audience segments through various digital channels (social media, search, display and e-mail or SMS).

Once it determined what was working and what wasn't, Albert scaled the campaigns, autonomously allocating resources from channel to channel, making content recommendations and so on.

For example, when it discovered that ads with the word "call"— such as, "Don't miss out on a pre-owned Harley with a great price! Call now!"—performed 447 percent better than ads containing the word "Buy," such as, "Buy a pre-owned Harley from our store now!" Albert immediately changed "buy" to "call" in all ads across all relevant channels. The results spoke for themselves.

If you are a small- or medium-business owner, there are so many ways AI can help you create brand value. A brand is a combination of rational and emotional benefits, but if you ask me, eventually all decisions we make are mostly influenced by our emotions. I can quote this from numerous personal examples.

In advertising, we often make pitches to clients in order to win their ad account. Usually when a company puts up its brand's ad business for a pitch, they shortlist and invite a number of agencies to present their ideas on how to tackle the issue stated in the pitch brief. Usually, the parameters for selection of the agency are quality of the idea, capability of the agency, team, experience in the category, credentials and their best work. Now if logic alone was to be the reason for choice, the biggest agencies should be winning most pitches simply because they have the best credentials, clients, experience and people. But in reality, that's not always the case.

Pitch after pitch, we've noticed that the selection of the agency is based on a factor outside of logical parameters.

The business is almost always decided based on the chemistry shared between the presenting agency team and the key decision makers in the client team.

There could be many reasons for this chemistry; the key decision maker may have worked with a senior agency personnel earlier or they could be socially connected or simply be friends, whatever the reason, if there's warmth in the relationship, it gets transmitted to everyone in the room during the course of the pitch presentation. The mood becomes lighter, jokes are cracked, hands are shaken warmly and almost always the meeting is followed by a tête-à-tête between the concerned individuals. The size of the agency becomes irrelevant, in fact, it won't matter if this was their first-ever assignment. Even an ordinary idea presented will show merit and eventually they bag the business, irrespective of what the others put up.

Why does this happen?

It is the emotional connect. The client team either unconsciously or deliberately, during the course of the presentations, decide WHO they want to work with. They take their decisions based on the people they see on the other side of the table. If for some reason, one has gotten off on a wrong foot, one can immediately sense the frigidity within the first few minutes of the presentation. The faces are unsmiling, the client team is distracted. The key decision makers are absent, sleeping or urging you to get over with it. Even a clutter-breaking idea cannot reverse the issue. Almost no questions are asked, everyone simply wants to get it over with as quickly as possible. When you find yourself in such an environment, the best advice for you is to cut your losses and beat a quick retreat.

To be bought, first you must be liked or likeable. To be liked by your customer you must do three things correctly:

1. Don't irritate them.
2. Be nice to them.
3. Connect with their deeper desires.

The first two points are simple and do not need explanation. The third point is what I would like to dwell upon. Here I'd like to go back to the advertising pitch case. Let us understand the entire process from the perspective of the head of the client team. Being a seasoned marketing veteran, she or he knows that success in their marketing effort would be an outcome of many variables, some that are known and can be controlled and others that are unknown and uncontrollable.

Little can be done about what is uncontrollable and unknown. A poor monsoon will dampen rural sentiment and will affect sales of almost all categories. An import ban levied by the government may scuttle their supply chain deliveries denying them with supplies of key components. And so on. These are matters of chance and luck and cannot be controlled by the person or the organization.

So, the decision maker decides to focus on those aspects of marketing that she or he can control, one of which is the advertising component. Now, most seasoned professionals know that your agency partner's work on your brand is only as good as the input and support you provide. So, the decision maker is confident that with their guidance, a capable and good agency partner, will eventually deliver the required output. What's important therefore is to have an agency that is tuned into the decision maker's thought process. Alignment ensures that the agency will eventually get it right. The only way a problem can occur is when the agency refuses to acknowledge the client's point of view and presents a different view, jeopardizing the overall marketing plan of the team. To a business head, this is allowing a controllable factor to become uncontrollable.

Which is why chemistry plays such an important role in B2B decision making. Business heads are looking for a team that's not just bright but also in tune with their thinking. A reason why they tend to prefer friends or people they have worked with in the past is, because there is a high level of comfort in the relationship that ensures they are in control of the output.

Similarly, customers tend to choose brands that they connect with, speaks their language, looks like them and shares a chemistry. Just like the way a business associate is chosen. Herein lies the challenge for mass brands. They aren't dealing with one individual but a sea of customers with myriad requirements and desires. How can it understand them all? How does a brand respond and offer solutions or even empathize with a wide swathe of needs and desires?

Here is where AI can help. AI clusters or classifies customers based on different needs captured in data. The system can then generate various options based on this data. Next, the AI can personalize the offers further based on the interactions with the customer and finally meet the customer's requirement by customizing a unique package. In this manner, AI can reduce the uncontrollable factors in a customer's purchase process and cause a favorable outcome for the brand.

Let me illustrate this with an example. Today, EdTech brands are proliferating as professionals and students embrace the online model of learning. Many of these EdTech companies have partnered with universities to provide certifications and degrees in different areas of study. Imagine an EdTech brand in this environment with a similar range of degrees to offer. Currently, the brand does not know the requirements of various customers who visit its site.

The home screen of the brand's website is a precious bit of virtual real estate that can accommodate only a limited number of courses. So, which courses should be put up? The obvious method is to place the most popular courses on the site or to display what's popular across the category. Unfortunately, this strategy is limiting as it will continue to attract the same kind of students, and will end up presenting the brand as not very different from the competition.

But suppose if you had an AI system that could offer courses based on the visitor's background, browsing habits and interest area? Now the home page becomes more dynamic and personalized to the requirements of different visitors. A good machine learning system will further track choices made by different profiles of customers and start creating patterns. It may conclude that IT professionals are keener to take up management courses and not just other technology courses. Senior managers prefer short modules or look for courses that provide a wide perspective with interactive sessions and opportunities to network. Mid-level managers seek prestigious courses that are flexible in period and modules, keeping with their busy schedules.

This will not just enable the brand to have better hit rate with its visitors but will enable it to customize and develop new course structures based on customer choice and behavior. AI has not just helped the brand connect better with its customers and net a wider audience but has also made the core product better, giving the brand a perceivable edge over other players, leading the change in the EdTech industry.

This kind of insight, personalization and customization is not restricted to online products and services only. It can be applied to most industries. If for example you own a car service garage, AI can help you understand what kind of repair work you tend to attract, it can help you identify other areas of your customer's needs that you can begin to solve by knowing their background. Offering personalization in your product mix, you can connect deeper with your client. For example, your AI system could indicate that some customers come to your garage only for critical task believing you are competent but expensive. By marrying this information with the other services provided, it could tailor unique introductory packages that are attractively priced and communicate these through messages or e-mails, inducing trials. The positive experience may encourage customers to change their opinion and consider your service more often, thereby increasing your net revenue per customer.

Let's consider that you're a start-up. Let's define that even tighter. You're actually on the first few days of your start-up journey. You have a fairly good idea of what your idea is and your product has been tested, received some traction and now you're looking to scale it up.

First, congratulations on getting this far. From my experience, 90 percent of start-up ideas fail at the concept stage itself. The fact that you are here is proof that you have it in you to go the distance. The first requirement about entrepreneurship is to have the ability to juggle multiple tasks at any instant of time. While you may have been busy multitasking at your earlier corporate avatar, you surely would have had a support system in place to take care of a lot of your noncore functions, such as admin, HR, payroll, legal and so on. Perhaps you also had a personal assistant or a team to support your effort.

But in entrepreneurship you do not have the luxury of a support system. You will definitely miss the support system that takes away the noncore activities, so that you can devote your full effort to what you are trained to do. While most entrepreneurs don't mind having to do those other activities, the issue is that these activities eat up a significant amount of an entrepreneur's precious time. Even the most efficient and effective entrepreneur can only do so much in a day. When the admin and support activities become urgent, they have to be attended to on priority, stretching work hours. Unfortunately, however hard and long you work, you may still end up missing an important investor's call or were distracted at a sales pitch because an urgent admin task was occupying your mind at that critical moment.

Perhaps this is why entrepreneurs are early adopters of technology and tech-enabled products. If you are one of this community, there's good news for you. The good news is that AI can handle a lot of those hygiene activities for you. A host of AI-enabled products can assist you with support services liberating you to focus on core activities.

Let's begin with the most basic yet the most essential of tools for a professional—your assistant. An efficient assistant multiplies your productivity. The characteristics of a good assistant is not merely efficiency or smartness or choice of words. A good assistant has the ability to *predict* a scenario and provide solutions for you to pick. Look back at your career, didn't your best assistants possess this quality?

The advantage with AI lies in its ability to predict. This aspect of AI is what makes it especially useful to you as your own AI-powered assistant. Siri and Google Assist are great tools that you can explore to lessen the burden on yourself. However, besides these there are a few other AI-enabled tools that can help you dramatically manage your entrepreneurial life. X.ai is one such tool. All you need to do is mark it on a cc of your every mail and a lot of your scheduling problems are taken care of. Some AI-based tools even link relevant files and e-mails to your calendar so that you have more than just a reminder, you have all the information available to you at the scheduled event, without having to dig through folders.

Nothing puts an entrepreneur off more than having to go through a huge folder of legal documents and paperwork. If the task was merely to read the document, it might still be manageable; however, knowing that one has to untangle a maze of legal lexicon written in a language that one is not accustomed to is quite deflating. The good part is that AI-based tools with the ability to scan through legal documents can present you with a summary of key points from the document, which is far more useful and actionable to a time-starved entrepreneur.

Does the word AI and machine learning conjure up images of coding and programming in your mind? Are you wondering if for a lot of this you may require to have coders, data scientists and engineers on board? The answer is no. A number of these tools require no coding, programming or technical knowledge on your part. Today, a lot of enterprises who are creating AI applications for businesses are perceptive and realize that for their applications to be genuinely useful, they must bridge over the technical aspects of coding and programming to have a broader appeal.

It's really commendable that a lot of these enterprises have not just democratized the use of AI and made it accessible to a global market but have gone one step further. They have enabled business across the world to customize it to their specific requirements without the need for coding. In these systems, libraries of pretrained neural networks exist, that an enterprise can use as a starting point to train and adapt for their own businesses.

Peltarion.com is a good place to explore. They have tutorials that first bring a visitor up to speed about the basics of AI and then provide you with information on how to devise an AI system for your business. They also provide a trial period during which one can get a handle on how to use tools to develop an AI model. From an image conversion model, to creating and understanding customer journeys to conducting and analyzing customer segments, there's a whole host of activities attuned to brand development that one can use. Don't let the fear of coding stymie your desire to use AI for brand building!

Similarly, there are online tools that are AI enabled, using which you can keep a constant tab of the consumer's voice. What conversations surround your brand in their social groups? What articles are being written about your brand? What are the complaints people have about your products?

If you are a fresh-off-the-block start-up and there's really not too much chatter around your brand, these tools can still give you a great idea about the category conversations and trends that are in your category. What is it that people are looking forward to? What is exciting for them about your category? Is there an ill-wind blowing your way? Are people moving out? Brandwatch is one such excellent tool that you could put into use for such great insights.

The last building block of any brand strategy is your competition. AI-enabled tools have that covered as well. Import.io gives you the ability to create your own reports by extracting data from other sites. Similarly, NGDATA's customer data platform enables you to understand your customer's journey, examining key decision points and Cortex gives you insights into your consumer's mind to help you develop unique content strategy different from competition. These are invaluable inputs to help you develop your own differentiated campaigns.

The essence of strategy is to understand your own strengths, know the category, customer and your competition. Once, this entailed owning a lot of physical assets and resources. Today, it's all within your grasp. You are only limited by your own imagination. All you need to do is break out of the box in your mind. Do not believe you are limited on any dimension. AI has enabled you to transcend those boundaries and arm yourself with all the information you need.

AI can do a lot, but it can't do everything and while functional and administrative tools will help you run more efficient campaigns, you may still have requirements for key positions in your organization. AI can take away the monotonous work, but you still need the creativity and lateral thinking ability of humans in core functions and across different aspects of your company. But there's good news for you here as well. AI may not be able to perform many human tasks but it definitely can help you in your search to recruit key people. Not just that, AI can help eliminate the repetitive elements in HR such as employee onboarding, payroll and so on. This empowers the HR function with quality orientation and also improves the efficiency of the HR department. HR requirements for a start-up are so dynamic with people requirements changing so rapidly, that sometimes you are looking for specialist skills while at other times, you could be looking for temporary staff. The environment today is rapidly evolving and it's difficult to have a traditional HR approach to handle diverse requirements. This is especially challenging for a small business owner wearing multiple hats, tackling multiple issues.

AI powers a number of HR platforms that can help you in your diverse requirements. From sites that will get you temp workers to specialist sites that can identify the unique skill you are seeking. It's all been worked out and it's all available for you.

Another important drain on your mind and resource is the threat of cyberattack. AI has this element of your business covered as well. Intelligent systems can now provide you with information on real-time threats. Recorded Future presents you with a wide suite of products and solutions that can keep you forewarned and therefore secure from potential threats. Cylance can help you eliminate false alarms as well as threats from malware because it has the ability to distinguish between malwares and regular programs. There are also a number of other intelligent applications that you could use for specific requirements you may have. Remember to keep an AI search bar open in your mind at all times and always use it when you feel the need, even as you look out for traditional solutions. Go beyond the areas I have listed in this book. Nothing is impossible for AI and you never know who has recently created what with your particular pain point in mind. You lose nothing by asking AI.

Now the playing field is leveled. Think big, be courageous and aim for the stars.

Chapter Summary

1. Emotions have a major role to play in all areas of decision making.
2. In B2B situations too, the chemistry shared with the vendor plays an important role in final selection.
3. AI applications offer a wide range of solutions for entrepreneurs.
4. AI can help cluster or classify customers based on needs, interactions and behavior, creating unique communication for all sets of audiences.
5. AI helps brand connect better by matching customer needs to the right product in your offering.
6. Available AI tools can take the place of an efficient assistant by predicting your activities and providing you with the necessary information to take correct decisions.
7. Use available AI tools in legal and HR functions to improve the overall efficiency of your start-up.
8. You can develop an excellent brand strategy by using AI. A whole host of products and services driven by AI can help you generate actionable consumer insights, get a heads up on the category and stay abreast of competitors.
9. Adopting AI can be achieved without the need for coding knowledge.
10. AI-driven cybersecurity solutions proactively secure organizations from cyber threats.

CHAPTER 7

Overview

A detailed and thorough brand strategy can be developed by deploying the tools outlined in the previous chapters. This chapter will explore the role of AI in creative development.

- An understanding of what is creativity.
- Applied creativity: Fertile ground for AI.
- The basic creative requirements for a brand.
- AI and brand nomenclature.
- Brand identity and AI.
- Developing websites using AI.
- Communication development using online AI tools.
- AI that develops creatives from textual inputs.

AI and Creativity

The composer Aiva's music album, "Genesis" is protected by copyright laws under France and Luxembourg's author rights society. Why this is unique? Because Aiva is an AI program. Aiva stands for Artificial Intelligence Virtual Artist. Aiva was taught how to compose classical music and learnt from the works of the great composers such as Mozart, Beethoven, Bach and others. Aiva then created a mathematical model to represent music and using this model developed "Genesis." Whether you like Aiva's music or not is a subjective matter, but what cannot be denied is that AI has now breached a unique bastion of human identity—creativity.

In the previous chapter, you have been exposed to tools and techniques to create the building blocks of your brand's strategy. Using this information, you should have a good idea of your category, competition and your consumer.

Business landscape today is extremely dynamic with nothing remaining constant for long. Paradoxically, change does not take place overnight. Change is not something that's a coordinated simultaneous shift—unless in the case of a pandemic-like situation. Change is the net result of a million little uncoordinated steps that take place sporadically across the world within a definite timespan. What makes them impactful is the fact that they occur with regularity and affect the functioning of work. All these tiny bits begin adding up. Change is like a predator, stealthily creeping up on its prey, inch by inch and then suddenly, in less than a fraction of a second, it's all over.

A cursory check of different companies in various industries across the world may not throw up indications of great change in progress. In fact, they could be following decades-old procedures even to this day. But that's the thing about change, it is something that's happening in the background that you don't notice, perhaps don't see or realize either. It is like the bamboo plant.

Nothing much happens for the first five years or so after you plant bamboo, except for tiny green shoots sprouting inches above the soil surface. You'd probably give up on it after a while and forget about it. Unseen and unknown to you, the bamboo is growing beneath the surface. After spreading its roots wide, strengthening its connections and anchoring itself, the bamboo suddenly begins to grow with a ferocity that will stun you! Before you know it, the bamboo has grown over 20 meters in height in a matter of 10 to 12 weeks only!

So, you mustn't scoff at the effort of one tiny company or a few ones. Neither should you point out to large factories and believe things are constant. Change is like that bamboo shoot; it's all happening beneath the surface. The seemingly uncoordinated efforts of thousands of tiny companies, each taking baby steps, all begin to multiply beneath the surface and then in the flash of an eye, everything changes. That factory that once stood is gone, those products you used are gone. The world has changed and those who didn't believe it would happen are left wondering *when* exactly did it happen?

Years ago, my agency worked on the account of India's largest TV manufacturer. This company had a host of brands that offered a range of TV sets with different features at varied price points. All these TVs were Cathode Ray Tube or CRT TVs, that is, they weren't the flat LED TVs of today. Before the current crop of LEDs became the in thing, there was a time when the TVs were LCD or plasma TVs. These TVs were large in size and expensive, beyond the reach of the average Indian, who was content to buy the traditional CRT TVs. Given the population of India and the rapid growth of satellite and cable TVs, the sales of CRT TVs were growing at a rapid pace. In order to keep up with the insatiable demand and also in a sign of hubris, this client of ours, bought out the CRT manufacturing factory of a large European company to become the world's largest TV manufacturer.

It was a short-lived achievement.

Our agency was called to pitch for their newly launched LED TVs. The client themselves didn't believe the category had any future, given the high price. Our pitch however was a radical one. We presented the idea that once these LED TVs were launched, people would find new ways to get rid of their old CRT TVs and adopt the new LED TVs.

It's been many years since we made that presentation, but I still remember the shocked silence that greeted us when we finished with our pitch. The owner and managing director of the company turned to ask me if I knew that they had just bought over the CRT facilities of their European rivals and were now officially the world's largest color TV (CTV) company. Without batting an eyelid, I told him that I was aware of the fact. I went on to clarify that we had made the presentation keeping the future in mind. And the future clearly belonged to LED TVs. Once people started buying them, their prices would fall, just like it happened with all electronics products and soon there wouldn't be space in our homes and in retail shelves for the old bulky outdated CTV.

The company had a different point of view. They didn't believe things would change and continued investing in CRT TVs and increased their efforts to push the products. But it proved to be futile. The company's decline was rapid and from a premier electronics player, it was reduced to a loss-making unit, which was eventually shut down in only a few years' time. This company, that had once spearheaded the country's evolution to color TVs, music systems and VCRs, refused to acknowledge the changing realities and paid a heavy price.

Therefore, accept and adapt to the changing times. You now have AI tools to help you with developing brand strategy, besides assisting you with your administrative tasks. Start putting them to use and lead the change in your industry or company.

AI can take you further than that too. AI can help you generate creative ideas as well.

A lot of people are surprised when I say this. People usually ask me how is that possible? How can AI be creative like humans? Isn't that totally right-brained? Something that AI could never achieve?

Creativity is such an intensely human trait; it is what differentiates us from other living beings and makes us unique. Valuations of companies and enterprises are often solely based on their creativity. How is it possible that creativity can be produced by an AI system? If so, does it spell doom for humankind?

These questions and perspectives are valid. There's acceptable logic in their questioning. Indeed, creativity is a uniquely human trait and machines haven't reached that level of sophistication as yet. So how am I saying that AI can be creative?

A common mistake that people make is tending to club everything that's not math or logic as being "creative." But not everything we term creative, *is creative*. There are actually two broad kinds of creativity.

Pure creativity and applied creativity.

Pure creativity is actually creativity. It's an artist's ability to create a form of art where there's no point of reference. It's an image that she or he conjures in her or his mind independently and uniquely. This image is not visible to anybody else. The artist then gives this image form in the shape of a movie, sculpture, book, story, painting, poem or innovation.

The rarer and more different this thought is, the higher it raises the boundaries of imagination and the better its execution, more is the value that gets attached to it. This is pure creativity.

The other form is applied creativity. This isn't about conjuring up a unique image that is invisible to the rest of the world. This is about taking an existing belief, idea or thought, regurgitating it and presenting it in an entertaining and refreshing manner. Advertising, pulp fiction, content writing, logo creation, jokes, the entire entertainment industry and many such industries fall under the aegis of applied creativity.

Applied creativity unlike pure creativity does not push the boundaries of human thought. Neither is it altruistic, like some forms of pure creativity are. Applied creativity has an objective attached to it, like getting the reader or viewer to take action that's linked with revenue generated for the creator. Take for example, the advertising that you see. Many of them are very good, they make you pause and reflect or even chuckle if the piece of communication tickles your funny bones. It's remarkably creative, you might say, which it is to some extent. The ad's creativity however is linked to an objective, which was to make you remember the brand and hopefully, act on the message to buy that brand. Having achieved its objective of creating awareness and interest, its task is done.

For having done this much, the agency that devised the ad is paid a fee. The agency's objective in creating the ad was primarily to get that reaction from you. Similar objectives drive the entertainment industry. Production houses spend millions of dollars to make superhero movies, investing huge amounts of money in special effects (SFX). While the end result is unique and brilliant, it is driven by a commercial objective—to sell more tickets and downloads on Over The Top (OTT) channels.

The same goes for books, plays, musicals and other industries linked to applied art.

While they also push boundaries, they do it in the limited arena of their craft and trade. Which is why all these industries have their own award ceremonies that celebrate their craftsmanship. Hollywood has the Oscars; advertising has its EFFIE and Cannes awards; and so on. These awards celebrate creativity and innovation in the limited arena of their trade raising the bar of craftsmanship each year in their respective industries.

In these industries there are a set of rules that are followed as best practices, and then there is a creative flourish that lends an extra edge to make some of the output unique and award-worthy. Which is why if you see the advertising industry as a whole, you may notice that a large proportion of all ads, be they press, TV, billboard or digital are run-of-the-mill mundane ads that aren't unique in their creativity. They essentially present the product or the solution or the image of the customer they are targeting and then state their proposition. It's not that they're deliberately not being creative, it's just that their research, data or experience may indicate that consumers are reacting better to such communication.

So, you could have a shampoo ad showing great tresses accompanied with image of the product connected by a simple line mentioning that this shampoo prevents hair fall or makes hair shiny and thick, because it has a special ingredient that strengthens hair. This approach plays out evenly in almost every category be it, personal care, lifestyle, B2B, wellness, real estate and others.

This is applicable to the film and entertainment industry as well, where a significant percentage of movies are based on the same old tried and tested formulae from the past: heist movies, action movies, war movies, horror, historical, musicals, and so on. The storylines in each genre are often predictable and vary only by a minor degree from each other, yet every one of these movie genres have a ready market of viewers.

It is in these fields of applied creativity that AI is increasingly finding a greater role to play. The use of a formula is a condition that is suitable for the application of AI.

Having provided the theoretical reason for the use of AI, let's pick up the threads of the entrepreneur's journey from the previous chapter.

As an entrepreneur or a business manager, you have developed your strategy and now you would be looking to execute your plan. In marketing, this stage entails the process of creative development. Assuming that the company is just a few weeks old, you will need to begin with a brand name and a logo.

AI can help you generate both, brand names and logos. Sites such as Namelix, Namesmith and many other sites can help you generate hundreds of options for your brand. Many of them use predictive AI that ask you the right set of questions and based on your feedback and its own learning, will generate options that are relevant and fit the brief.

If you aren't clear about what is a brief: A brief is a critically important document that succinctly captures the current situation and sets the expectation for the output.

In order to help yourself identify the right name for your brand, you must create a brief for the task.

Should the brand name be connected to the category? For example, Petronas, Petrobras. Or can it be an unconnected but catchy name? For example, Google.

Do you have a role model, aspiration or vision that the brand name must capture? For example, Tesla, Nike and Virgin.

Should the brand name have something you've built in the past to be connected with it? For example, Nescafe, Nestea.

Do you prefer short single words or are you fine with multiple words?

Are you looking to abbreviate a name? For example, Adidas.

Do you want to stand for some human value? For example, Reliance.

Generating brand names is easy and the AI-based sites will help you achieve that. The hard part is selecting the right one. Here is where a well-written, clear brief plays an important role. Writing down what exactly you seek from the brand name, will help you get clarity about the requirement in your mind. With a good brief, words that best capture your dreams, aspirations and efforts would already have started forming in your mind. Now look again at all the names that have been generated, through the filter of the brief. A few will stand out. Sleep over the shortlist. Get them vetted by team members, family and friends—people whose judgment you trust. And then go for it.

Now you have your brand name, the next requirement would be the logo. Once again, a plethora of AI-based online sites can help you with this. Logomaster, Logoai, Brandmark and so on are a few of the logo development sites you could visit. All of these have their own unique approaches. Some ask you minimal questions, others take you through a series of pointed questions that refine the process and provide you with relevant options. All options provided are usually editable so you can further improvise and make changes to create the logo that matches your requirements. The entire process of logo development could take anywhere from 10 minutes to about an hour. Imagine, under an hour you can have a personalized logo for your brand!

Once again, it is important to have clear brief before embarking on the logo creation process. Your brief should cover the following areas:

What is the style theme you have in mind for your logo? Professional, casual, fashionable, luxury? Style is important because it will cue the brand's personality, tone and attitude to the customer. There are some thumb rules you must follow when deciding on your logo style. Financial or professional service brands must be reassuring and cue dependability. Money and professional advice are serious business and people don't feel comfortable with a casual-looking logo or a funky logo dishing out advice for one's life savings. To them, such logos could convey a flippant, shallow brand.

Professionals may argue that one's track record should be reassuring enough. The problem is no consumer wants to be the exception, preferring to err on the side of caution. Similarly, a luxurious-looking logo would also be misplaced in such circumstances. People don't mind paying top dollars for the best professional service, but they want to believe that their money is being put to good use such as having the best team and technology to manage their money and not spent on items of indulgence.

What are the colors you have in mind? People link colors with categories. Green signals nature, freshness and life. Yellow for hope, brightness and positivity. Blue and black represent professionalism and calm. Red is a symbol of dynamism, enterprise and change. White represents peace, tranquility and serenity. While these aren't watertight compartments, it's good to bear them in mind in order to avoid basic mistakes. So, if you own a seafood restaurant, blue would be a good color to use instead of red, just as a fresh food logo in whites and blacks would be a poor fit indeed and so on.

Sometimes an image, symbol or icon adds value to a logo. The paint industry in India in its early days had famous mascots and icons representing their brands. The paint company Goodlass Nerolac (now Kansai Nerolac) had a tiger called Goody as a mascot on all their paint cans. Its rival, Asian Paints carried the illustration of Gattu, a young boy with a paint brush, created by the great cartoonist R. K. Laxman, on theirs. The purpose of these mascots was to make their cans easily identifiable to the painters, who purchased paint on behalf of the customers. The painters were uneducated and identified the brands purely on the basis of these mascots. As India progressed and the education levels among painters increased, the mascots lost their relevance and soon a time came when both companies decided to do away with their respective mascots.

These logo-generating sites offer you the option of including such symbols, emoticons and images that you can use as a trademark going forward. It is for you to think over the applications of the logo, the users and influencers and decide if you need one.

You also need to give thought to the font you would like to use. Fonts convey the essence and personality of the brand. When we designed the logo for Mahindra First Choice, a pioneer in the used car market in India, we consciously created the logo using a thick font in order to convey the trust that the brand signified in an otherwise unorganized industry. On the other hand, when designing the logo for ATG—a new entity in the global off-highway tire category, we used futuristic fonts to convey the international pedigree of the brand. Through their size, shape, serif or sans-serif identity, fonts speak to your customers on behalf of your brand. They are the soul of the logo, get them right and you have struck gold.

Lastly, evaluate the need for a baseline. Ideally baselines should be attuned to your brand's proposition or to the mission statement. A baseline is not mandatory. In fact, I'm of the firm opinion that unless you have a baseline that is provoking and focused, it's better not to have one at all. Famous baselines aren't created by accident. They stem from the fundamental core of the brand belief. Nike's "Just Do It" isn't just a slug line, it's a philosophy that reflects the brand and its outlook to life. Similarly, the Indian behemoth, Reliance India Limited's baseline of "Growth is Life" resonates with the company's relentless drive to keep pushing the boundaries of growth, making its stock a darling of the Indian investor. Many lives have been transformed, thanks to the returns the company and its stock provided over the years. Never include a baseline that's bland and there simply because you needed one. In communication, less is better. Nobody remembers 99 percent of baselines, simply because they meant nothing. My advice to entrepreneurs is do not create a baseline right away. Wait. The business will settle down and after a while you will have clarity about what your brand means to your customer. Capture that truth in a line and you have a winning baseline. If it isn't there keep waiting and checking.

Once you have a rough image of your expectations from your logo in mind, begin the process of online logo generation, follow the steps and use your mental image as a reference to help refine the process. At the end of it you should have a logo that should be close to the image you had in mind. Now you have a face for your brand.

I have heard a lot of brand managers and entrepreneurs lament over the logos of their brands. They complain at times that it is outdated or that it means nothing to the consumer, or that the fonts are too thin or too thick or the colors are too wrong. In my opinion a logo has no meaning, unless an organization and team puts meaning behind it. Meaning is the delivery of real value to the customer—tangible or intangible. When this happens, logos start meaning something to people. Then it doesn't matter if the font is thin or thick or colors are too bright or dull. The customer finds meaning in it. In isolation a logo is nothing but a carefully crafted image, while you may put all your skills and make it look good, it will still lose to an inferior design, if it doesn't add value to the customer's life. Contrary to popular sentiment, feel free to constantly improve your logo, update it and modernize it from time to time. These are signs to customers that your company is busy improvising its products and services. Remember brand equity is not calculated by the beauty of a logo's design, but by the difference the brand has made to the customer. The more valuable the difference the greater the brand's value.

The important point here is that action trumps look. I've seen companies get bogged down in designing their logo, spending so much time in deliberations and iterations to get it absolutely right that they lose the market opportunity and let customers slip away. Of what use is a beautiful logo that has no customer to talk to? So, while brands must aim for the best, it must be time-bound. A logo that's achieved 90 percent of expectation should be good to go. Keep iterating as you go along and you will be in a far better place.

Today, besides a logo and a brand name, there's one more property that's a must-have before a brand launch. That's the website.

While the role of websites has been increasing in prominence and importance in recent years, the COVID pandemic has turned this important tool into an absolute essential element of a brand's building blocks. The pandemic has turned people's buying behavior on its head. Without the option of going out, people were forced to turn to the net to get information about products and services that they were planning to purchase. In such a scenario, websites are the first place people visit, to know more about brands, companies and how they have been rated by other customers. For all product categories, handicrafts, personal care and lifestyle products the websites have become the primary, if not the sole source of information, credibility, assurance and offers. While the pandemic and its memories may fade away, this behavior of the consumer is here to stay. Which makes having a website, especially a website with a clearly defined objective, a must for brands.

Once, designing and developing a website was a costly and time-consuming affair, but not anymore. Indeed, it is due to AI. Sites such as Wix, Shopify, Bookmark and many other AI-enabled website building site, are one-stop shops that can help you create a stunning website for your brand without needing any knowledge of development, coding or designing. Many of these sites use predictive AI techniques enabling you to distill your thought process and provide the right inputs and direction necessary to develop a great website. What's more, you can build any kind of a website you may require, be it an e-commerce site or a food blog or a travel site. These sites are interactive, easy to use and provide you with lots of design options too.

Then again, you need to have clarity about the objectives and the content strategy for the site. Once you have this in place, all you need is to select the website that best reflects your brand's personality, modify it to include your content and after a bit of adjustments, you are ready to roll!

It may sound incredible, but the truth is that today you can create a brand name, design a logo and get your website up and running all in a day's time. Start in the morning and by evening you're ready for business. This was unimaginable even a few years back. But thanks to AI, you don't need to lose a single day's business. You also don't need large teams, experts and professional designers and expensive software to do this. You aren't hostage to the schedules of others, or stuck having to choose between limited options. These are the doubts that gnaw away at an entrepreneur, who mostly has to manage all of this alone. AI has put an end to a lot of the limitations that entrepreneurs had to live with. It's now up to you and your enterprise to get yourself up and running. With a little bit of help from your friend, AI.

With a website in place, your shop is now open for business. Having done this much, you would be feeling a rush of adrenalin coursing through your veins. This is a wonderful feeling; it reinforces your self-belief and the confidence with which you embarked on the journey. While this is a great feeling, be prepared for the time when this initial flush will begin to drain away and expected footfalls and clicks fail to materialize. These are times when you need to keep the momentum going. To begin with, inform everyone in your circle about your venture. This includes family, friends, associates, network and connections. Engage with them on call, messages and mail, tell them clearly what you do, your products, solutions and so on. Don't overthink this step. Don't tell yourself, "Hey I'm still work-in-progress, let me wait a bit." Or "Let my business get big." Or "Come on, nobody cares" or worse, "Nobody will help" and "I will be laughed at."

I cannot tell you how wrong these negative thoughts are. As an entrepreneur myself, I have battled these questions on numerous occasions. And every one of those times I was happy to be proven wrong. People in your circle genuinely care for you. They want to and definitely will help you, if they can.

The universe wants you to succeed. All it asks of you is to put in your best efforts. Your heart, soul and every iota of energy you can muster must go into this thing that you are creating. Next, keep that effort on, day in and day out. Don't ever be wracked by self-doubt, don't take your foot off the pedal and don't ever stop. Just keep at it, irrespective of time and one day, you will definitely see results. What might take you by surprise is that the results may appear in the places you least expected. At other times, your actions could find you unique and life-altering partnerships. All of it is the universe's way of acknowledging your unstinting effort and dedication to your idea.

This is not an accident, neither is it a matter of luck. If you put in effort and importantly, let people know of the progress, however infinitesimal it may be, people begin to take notice of your work and keep you in mind. They're watching you and cheering for you, albeit silently. They want you to succeed, as much as you do. If they're not getting back to you initially, it is because perhaps in all the noise surrounding us, they simply haven't heard you, or registered your voice, or noticed your efforts, or aren't in a position to help you, even though they dearly want to. Perhaps despite their best intentions, they don't have the right project for you at that particular moment. Which is why continuous and consistent effort in communication needs to back every idea. Be mulish here, don't think too much. In fact, don't think at all! Simply do. Take one step at a time. Especially in your darkest moments, (and there *will* be plenty of those) soldier on. Then one day out of nowhere, bam! You will get a tiny little lead.

That should be a good enough starting point. Grab it and move ahead.

To begin with, inform your family, friends, associates, network and connections personally and on social media. These channels are free, so sign up, put up your company page and begin posting and sharing information about your company, brand, the solution it provides and any offers you may have from time to time. While there are numerous social media channels, please select only those relevant to your business, do not dissipate your energy and effort in hammering away at channels that do not have your relevant audience. Create a calendar of activity that covers all areas—products, offers, new launches, festival greeting, special occasions, as well as general posts that reflect the brand's views on current events and topics. Follow a regular schedule for posting on these sites. Today AI-powered tools will actually schedule and post automatically on these sites. All you need to do is to plan your activity calendar and generate the content, for which again AI sites exist!

This simple act is the first sign that your company, brand and efforts are sincere and have a plan powering it. All these tiny bits of effort are what eventually add up and convert awareness into interest, desire and finally action from your customers. Your initial customers will always be people who you know personally. Getting them onboard will not just help you take off but also provide you with invaluable information and data that you can use to improve your offering.

Informing people even on social media channels and through small local promotions requires you to develop different pieces of communication relevant to those channels. For social media, you need posts; for local promotions, you may need banners or leaflets or press advert designs. For business communication, you may need a brochure or a power point presentation beautifully designed to impress your audience. All of this requires careful thought, planning and execution.

While you can do the thinking and planning, you could perhaps face a roadblock when it comes to designing the creative for your communication collateral. Typically, you will need the skills of an art director and a content or copy writer to present your plan in a creative manner that jumps out of the clutter and connects with your audience.

Unfortunately, getting a talented pair to work on your requirements with regularity could be a stumbling block for you. In my interactions with entrepreneurs, I've realized that very often this is a huge pain point for them. Entrepreneurs instinctively understand the critical role good communication plays in their business efforts. But getting the right communication support is difficult for them. Given that the size of business is very small, putting resources on it is not remunerative for large communication agencies, unless of course they charge a huge fee, which is unaffordable for a budding enterprise. The other option for an entrepreneur is to work using freelancers. However, identifying the right freelancer is a time-consuming task, moreover freelancers often work on a very tight framework, with little scope for changes and corrections. This rigidity could be unsuitable for the dynamic nature of a start-up and the entrepreneur could end up wasting a lot of his or her time in correcting the draft or chasing the freelancer for the delivery of important creative to meet business deadlines.

Often, the end result is one of two things: The entrepreneur ends up spending far more time, money and effort in creating the desired output or has to make do with whatever piece of communication is received.

Both of these are suboptimal solutions. Regretfully, many entrepreneurs frequently find themselves in such unenviable positions.

But today they have alternatives. A number of AI-enabled online sites offer entrepreneurs the option to create their own communication material. These sites such as Canva for example, have an easy-to-use format with a plethora of template options, with which an entrepreneur can develop communication material suited to the brand. The templates on these sites offer a wide variety of styles, designs and font options, with earmarked position for copy and visuals, which the entrepreneur can suitably modify for their own particular needs. The process is simple, structured and helpful. The visitor simply needs to follow the steps on the site that will guide them to creating their desired output. From social media posts to invitations and posters, there's a lot one can create on sites like these.

For entrepreneurs who are rushed for time and do not even have a few hours to spare or lack the creative acumen to use AI-powered tools to design their own creatives based on templates, newer AI-enabled tools are available that convert text-based input into creative output. Now, entrepreneurs can simply enter their requirements as text into a brief format and will receive options for the creatives in a matter of minutes.

How does this work?

As I have stressed earlier in the book, the essence of any good communication is the creative brief. A good creative brief distills the thought process and captures only the important elements an intelligence needs to know to generate a good piece of creative. A well-written creative brief is half the job done, when it comes to developing creative output.

The characteristics of a good brief are:

Objective clarity: Who is the communication for and what is the desired outcome.
Brevity: Say only what you must.
Focus: On the specific task at hand.
Comprehensive: Cover all aspects of the requirement, including technical details.

A good brief captures all the critical elements that are essential inputs for a creative team to understand what has to be conveyed specifically in terms of message, visuals, contact details, logo, copy points and other mandatory. It also specifies where the creative will appear, the size, material and shape of the output. All these tiny details are important. Without this information, the creators will not know where and how this creative output would be viewed. Without clarity, the entire effort could be wasted. For example, if the final output required is a social media post, the creative team not knowing this, could develop a long copy ad. Since social media posts have limitations on length of the copy, this ad would get rejected, wasting the effort put into its creation. Adverts without a call for action may not lead to any calls or website clicks. A promotion that fails to mention the address of the event would serve no purpose. Using a visual in the creative is pointless if the substrate that the creative will appear on is not conducive for displaying visuals. Packaging design brings a different level of complexity altogether, without specifying which, there's no point in starting the task at all. Simple as these may sound, communication is replete with instances of huge losses caused due to these glaring errors.

On BICO, Brief In, Creative Out, a text to visual creative generation platform, currently under development, great emphasis is laid on the brief. It's an extremely granular process that captures all the elements that go into creating a great brief. It pushes the writers of the brief to think through their requirements and specify all aspects. Once the brief is captured, BICO's AI, which is intuitive, understands the brief by breaking it down into its many components. Its natural language processing (NLP) ability places the brief in the right context, evaluating countless similar communication in a matter of seconds. Once it understands the context and the category, it digs deeper into the messaging requirements. It identifies keywords for the headline and begins intelligently crafting options. Once the options are approved, the AI identifies the right images for the headline selected and composes the final creative.

Peppertype.ai is a content generation site that uses AI to develop creative content ideas that brands can uses in various spheres of marketing and Designs.ai converts text to video outputs using AI. The proliferation of these AI-enabled creative development tools have magically unshackled brands from the constraints of the past enabling them to communicate dynamically with their consumers across different channels and formats.

Chapter Summary

1. Communication is the dynamo that powers enterprise. If you have to sell, you have to tell.

2. AI is a game changer in the applied creativity fields of advertising, movie making, entertainment, and so on.

3. Entrepreneurs have traditionally found it difficult to get quality creative solutions for their needs having to either pay a high price or suffer from poor-quality vendors.

4. Today, entrepreneurs can develop any kind of creative requirement online, thanks to the power of AI.

5. Any creative process whether AI or human uses the same process of garbage in garbage out, therefore it is critical that entrepreneurs first write down the brief for each creative output that they seek.

6. Name generator sites use AI to provide entrepreneurs with countless options for brand names.

7. AI-driven logo design websites can help entrepreneurs construct beautiful logos in minutes.

8. AI-powered website builders create websites for entrepreneurs in a matter of hours without the need to know designing, coding or development.

9. A number of AI-enabled sites provide templates, using which entrepreneurs can build their specific creative units.

10. On some AI-enabled creative development sites, one can simply type in a written brief and receive a creative output in a matter of minutes.

CHAPTER 8

Overview

Having detailed out the process of understanding and communicating with your customers in the previous chapters, this chapter covers aspects of customer engagement where AI can be put to use.

- Why customers matter to entrepreneurs.
- Efficient processes alone do not create customer engagement.
- The difficulty in managing customers in a connected world divided by time zones.
- Using AI-enabled chatbots as a first line of communication.
- Using predictive AI for better consumer engagement.
- Personalization through AI to create customer delight.
- The role of AI-driven Customer Data Platforms (CDPs) in managing complex sets of customer relationship.
- Optimizing opportunities using AI-enabled CDPs.

AI in Customer Engagement

Marvel, the comic book publisher found a unique way to promote the launch of "Secret Empire" a part of its summer crossover series. Through Marvel's chatbot, fans could converse with their friendly neighborhood superhero, Spidey himself. The success of the program prompted Marvel to launch similar events to coincide with the launch of "Guardians of the Galaxy" and other superhero characters subsequently. The popularity and high level of engagement that fans had with the bot heroes, led Marvel to team up with Hong Kong Disneyland to create a Marvel superhero experience, which was a resounding success in terms of gaining users. Today Marvel's chatbots form an integral part of its consumer engagement process as Marvel Comics' chatbot allows fans to converse with some of their favorite marvel superheroes and become part of the story.

Entrepreneurship is unique because few other endeavors in life can match the range of emotional crests and troughs that this experience puts one through. Nothing equals the adrenalin rush that courses through one's veins as one surmounts obstacle after obstacle to achieve one's goals. An entrepreneur knows no vacation, is restless even during a holiday and is frustrated by any event that keeps her or him away from their all-consuming passion—their start-up.

An entrepreneur is always switched on, is usually the first one in and the last to leave work every day. Truth is, even when away, they're plugged in. Now, there are many good arguments that recommend the need for professionals and entrepreneurs to inculcate the ability to switch off from work and relax. All of these are excellent advice. While most entrepreneurs indeed wish they possessed that ability to switch off at will, the passion of running a start-up is all-consuming and many entrepreneurs prefer not to be disconnected from their work. To an entrepreneur work may be stressful but it is also the panacea. It may consume the individual, but nothing can match the high that it provides.

If you were to ask an entrepreneur what their secret wish would be, many may say that their only desire is to multiply themselves and always remain connected with their customers. Solving the customer's problems, finding ways around difficult obstacles and doing things more efficiently is what drives entrepreneurship. It's almost as if entrepreneurs want to be clued into their customers and prospects, 24x7, 365 days of the year.

There's a reason why they feel that way. If you've ever had a problem with a product and complained about it, you would have experienced a difference in how an employee tackles your problem versus the way the owner tackles it. The employee's response would be to follow protocol and guidelines. The response to your problem would also be constrained by the working hours and geographical limitations of the company. Now contrast that with an owner's approach. If the owner gets to hear about your problem, she or he would move heaven and earth to solve it.

I have a very interesting personal experience that illustrates this point. Years ago, I had purchased a time-share vacation from a subsidiary company of one of India's largest conglomerates. The fact that they were giving a free video camera was a big reason for me to go for it. I was planning a vacation with my young family—the first for us after a long period of work. I had conjured up dreams of a vacation in one of their wonderful resorts, filming my young son, enjoying his vacation. I had paid up and was told that the Handycam would reach me in two weeks' time. With this in mind, I booked the resort and made my travel arrangements accordingly. Two weeks went by and no Handycam came, my reminders to the salesperson and then his boss only got me some standard responses. A few more weeks went by, in which time I got more and more frantic trying to reach them. But by now the entire team, once so attentive, had stopped responding to my calls.

With only a week left to go, I was crestfallen. The absence of the Handycam had taken away the joy from my impending vacation. My family tried to console me but to no avail. In desperation I searched and got my hands on the e-mail address of the Chairman of the conglomerate, a highly respected gentleman, considered to be an industry thought-leader, and wrote him an e-mail, explaining what had transpired, mentioning my anguished state of mind.

Having sent the e-mail, I had little expectations and had resigned myself to a vacation without the Handycam.

Imagine my surprise when I promptly received a wonderfully empathetic letter from the Chairman apologizing for the anxiety caused to me and assuring me that the Handycam would be delivered to me, before I left for my vacation. True to the great man's word, I received it the very next day! I also received a series of calls from the sales executive and his team apologizing for not acting on my plaints. While the videos of my young child's first vacation remain dear to me, the Chairman's humane response and lesson is deeply ingrained in my heart.

It tells us how much importance business owners place on their reputation. To the owner of a U.S. 20 billion dollar enterprise, the feelings and emotions of a single customer goes beyond mere economics. This gentleman firmly believed, "Not a single promise made by my brand, however infinitesimal it may be, should be broken." Indeed, this is how he built a global conglomerate. He genuinely felt my pain, felt personally responsible and responded to it with care and sensitivity, displaying the same commitment that any entrepreneur would display to their customers. What a contrasting response this was from his highly qualified and talented employees. For them, response to customer issues is part of a Standard Operating Procedure (SOP). If the process fails, it's a technical issue for the concerned department to solve. They did not believe that it was their job to solve a customer's problem.

This is one personal example. There are countless other instances. Geography and time-zone issues ensure that it is virtually impossible for someone in California to talk to someone in India during working hours to solve an issue that may have arisen. If both sides stick to their working hours and try and resolve the matter on mail, it's simply going to take that much longer. And what if the solution required is immediate? Imagine the frustration of the customer sitting in Mumbai or San Francisco waiting for the other to begin their day!

This is the reason why entrepreneurs want to be clued on 24x7, 365 days of the year. They realize the possibility of a customer or prospect trying to reach out for help but between office bureaucracy and employee apathy, the opportunity could be missed. The entrepreneur also knows that nobody cares for their business or customer as much as they do and so take on additional work and stress to attend to it themselves. The same cannot be demanded of employees who are simply following rules.

Entrepreneurs can now breathe easy because the critical element of customer engagement is something that entrepreneurs can now safely leave in responsible hands. Hands that are always available 24x7, and not be tired out either. Their representative will always be available to sort out their customer's problems and find them solutions irrespective of time zones or work hours. It's all possible.

AI makes it possible!

Thanks to AI, enterprises can be responsive to their customers round the clock and in multiple languages and through various channels of communication. That's because in this digital age it's the consumer's prerogative on how they want to reach out to you. It could be on e-mail, a messenger app, on your website, a helpline number or a tweet. There are many ways a customer or prospect may try to reach you. Remember if your customer or prospect is trying to get through to you, it means you are high priority for her or him. It's the highest state of involvement with your brand that you will ever find your customer to be in. It is the moment of truth. If you connect with them at this moment, chances of landing a sale or better, a customer for life is certain. Miss that moment and your customer would have cooled off by the time you get back to him and perhaps even bought your rival brand.

Another example from my years in advertising comes to mind. The global creative head of our agency was visiting the Mumbai office. The team had pulled out some of the best work to show him. Having reviewed them, he asked to see some of the work that was currently under execution. Proudly, the team pulled out the work that was being actioned for a global consumer electronics giant. This company was bullish on the color TV segment and taking advantage of the Soccer World Cup that was on, had launched a campaign highlighting their prompt service in the soccer-crazy city of Kolkata, which was a key market for the brand.

The team had crafted a snazzy ad and punchy headline that underscored the speed of the company's service. The copy spoke of how the brand was committed to the city's love for soccer and had constituted a special, after-sales service force that would ensure a technician reach the customer's house under an hour to sort out any issues customers may have with their TV, thus enabling uninterrupted viewership of the soccer world cup. Everyone was really pumped up about the campaign that was to be released as full-page adverts on the front pages of the city's popular Bengali and English papers. The adverts were in the process of being couriered to the respective publications, as they were scheduled to appear over the next few days.

This global creative director, an Englishman, famously known never to mince his words, took one look at the advert, then at the pumped-up faces facing him, raised his eyebrow and asked, "Do any of you play soccer?" A few replied in the affirmative. To them he asked, "Do you know the duration of an average soccer game?" "90 minutes," came the prompt reply. "Right!" he continued, "So let's assume that half-an-hour into the game, the TV conks off. This distraught soccer-crazy fan, rushes to call your brand's helpline, on the city's choked network. Assuming he gets through immediately and assuming they respond as promised and assuming they have an unoccupied person, assuming he beats the heavy Kolkata traffic to reach the customer's house in an hour's time, assuming that the technician is a gold medalist and assuming he miraculously completes the repair in 5 minutes only..." He paused at this juncture, to let the full weight of his next few words sink in, then asked, *"How much of the remaining match do you suppose that roomful of soccer-crazy fans would get to watch?"*

A stunned silence followed as the bitter truth reverberated across the room. The senior most executives rushed out, some to call the client, others to stop the ad. The lesson stayed with many of us for years. In fact, it's as relevant today as it was, back then.

There's a huge difference in saying we are responsive to actually being responsive. Responsiveness is getting back to the customer when it matters to them. Anything after that is just bureaucracy. Another important lesson from this episode is to always evaluate the promise being made to the customer, hopefully before making it.

If your product fails to deliver on its promise or fails to deliver in the moment of the customer's need, your brand has broken the faith your customer had placed on it, which is irreparable damage. The customer will never turn to you again and when she or he finds a better option, they will definitely switch from your brand.

AI can help you be responsive to your customer. It can engage with your customer, talk to them, provide them with options, educate them, teach them, demonstrate to them and finally escalate the matter to a human member of your team. However, it is your responsibility to design a practical process for this. Remember AI is only a wonderful tool that you can put to use, it can do a lot but, crafting the customer engagement process, is still your job.

You need to examine the different touchpoints of your customer, where, how and what exactly could be the multitude of reasons the customer is reaching out to you. From the earlier chapters, you have the tools to give you granular information about these aspects. You also have the AI tools to help you solve a large part of the responsive strategy. What you need to do is make the linkages and connect the dots. Create and train the AI tool and put in place the human intervention areas. Remember, once in place, the AI will keep adapting as it learns from real-life cases, it will become smarter and offer better solutions as time passes.

There are three clear advantages that AI brings to your customer engagement experience.

Responsiveness

Through AI-enabled chatbots, your brand can be accessible to customers around the world 24x7. With its self-learning abilities, chatbots are excellent at handling a lot of the initial queries and issues that customers face. A recent report indicates that over 50 percent of customers acknowledge having interacted with chatbots and close to 50 percent of them were satisfied with the solution provided by the chatbot.

Predictiveness

AI tools are continuously updating themselves with every interaction they have with the customer. If a matter is escalated and a new solution is incorporated by the human agent, the AI internalizes this and learns, so the next time round no human intervention is required for a similar problem. Also, because it can cluster consumer segments, it has the ability to pull out solutions that it believes were useful to people with a similar profile, and from the response, it can further divide the audience making solutions more granular.

This has another great advantage. AI can, through its predictive nature, fix problems before they arise. With AI's ability to keep learning and improving, it begins to see patterns in common problems and builds linkages. This information provides insights on recurring problems to help begin the process of developing solutions for the same. Similarly, if the problem is recurrent in a product, AI can identify the customers who bought that same batch or model and predict that they are likely to experience similar problems. With this information, companies can take preemptive measures such as product recall or send e-mails informing customers of the steps to take to solve the problem. Companies can go a step further by proactively offering free service checkups that corrects the problem even before it raises its head.

AI can also indicate if a customer is not using a product properly. This is extremely useful since quite often, improper use of a product results in its damage, leading to a negative customer perception. By preempting this, AI begins to build customer faith in the brand. Taking it a step further, AI can also help customers get more out of their brand by educating them on all its features. Typically, brands offer a plethora of benefits; however, they tend to focus on communicating a limited number in order to prevent confusion. AI helps customers get more from their existing products, by engaging with them on a regular basis and informing them of the supplementary benefits over time. If your computer can detect that you're not using a lot of its features, it can trace your pain points and advise you at critical moments about the existence of those features and how, by using them, you could save time, money and effort.

Personalization

Imagine you have purchased a mobile phone recently and now you're scouring the net for some high-end ear buds that complement your phone. What if you encounter a situation when an ear bud brand calls out to you by name, mentions the phone you've bought, gives you stats on the fact that maximum people with your phone buy the buds of that brand. It explains why it's the preferred choice, provides you with payment options and also selects a bud in the color of your choice!

Chances are that you would go with that brand, right? AI does this. It ensures your brand recognizes your customer. Your brand gets to treat each customer individually, catering to their specific likes and preferences.

AI helps you understand your customer better and personalize solutions for them, improving the relationship and helping you make a customer for life.

It doesn't end there. The AI can tell if this customer had purchased the same brand of smart phone earlier, it can bring out records to identify if the customer's earlier phone was brought into a service center for repair. From those records it can glean the age of the phone, the kind of repair that was done on it. If for example, the phone was brought in because its screen was damaged, the AI can offer screen protection products to the customer or throw in an extended warranty. If the earlier phone was registered as having been stolen, the AI could offer an insurance option. If the customer behavior indicated that she or he liked to replace their phones within a year, the AI could provide buy-back options for the phone with the planned model for the coming year. It could also register the customer for a privileged sneak-peak of the planned models for the next year and begin engaging the customer with interesting tidbits of information, keeping them hooked to the brand.

It's no wonder that Microsoft believes that by 2025, 95 percent of all customer interactions will be through channels supported by AI.

To enable a consistent and unified set of marketing activities, you need a CDP. According to Gartner, a CDP is a marketing system that unifies a company's customer data from marketing and other channels to enable customer modeling and optimize the timing and targeting of messages and offers. Basically, now you have a single place where all your customers interactions can be integrated, segmented, studied and analyzed, based on which, marketing can design unique programs for different customer sets who are at different stages of interaction with the brand. With AI powering a number of CDPs, this enables brands to carry out vast sets of valuable conversations simultaneously with customers, offering an increasing range of possible solutions, all on a real-time basis. This process is fast emerging as a must-have for brands not just in the B2B space but also on the B2C space.

The advantages of an AI-driven CDP are multifold. Imagine you have a jewelry company, your AI-enabled CDP will help you engage with multiple consumers simultaneously, customizing different selling strategies depending on the stage of purchase they may be in. For example, for males between 25 and 35, the system can intuitively recommend engagement or marriage rings. To women of the same age group, it could recommend the trending products in workwear and in casual wear. Based on the interest shown, visitors could be provided with information on the number of other customers viewing or trying out the product virtually, it could recommend a matching pair of earrings too. What's more, by understanding the visitor's profile better, it could inform her or him about which of their friends bought what products on the site.

Going forward, it may be able to connect the jewelry with the other recent fashion and clothes the visitor may have purchased by pulling out data from the consumer's purchase data. Based on this information, it could recommend specific products and categories that match the visitor's wardrobe. The AI could also begin to classify the overall style of different consumers and further break down the style into specific styles for different occasions and based on that information, make suggestions and recommendations. It could also understand the credit rating of the customer and tailor make on-the-spot, finance packages that are simply too good to resist.

Marketing is nothing more than wearing down your customer's resistance to purchasing your brand. If the customer is interested, then all other factors are merely stumbling blocks that prevent the thrill of acquiring a new product. A lot of times these barriers exist only in the minds of the customers and brands are unaware of the multiple reasons for not converting. It's simply shrugged off as being not convincing enough. The truth is that the more you engage with your customer, the more you understand her or him and the better are the options you present to them. The more offers you make, the happier the customer is and the more they will begin opening up about the barriers for purchase with you. The more of these you are able to take care of, the closer you will connect with the customer and finally when you have eliminated all obstacles, you will have a sale.

In the physical world, owners, entrepreneurs and business managers have been doing this for ages. Standing in markets, fairs and exhibitions talking to prospects and coaxing them to buy one by one. Today AI-enabled CDP permits brands to conduct multiple conversations simultaneously. ActionIQ, Amperity, Blueconic are some of the companies offering solutions in this space. Entrepreneurs need to develop their objectives and process and evaluate and adopt the right CDP to engage at the next level with their customers.

AI comes integrated into a number of customer relationship management (CRM) tools as well; Salesforce Einstein, Zoho and many others offer AI-enabled solutions for better customer management. Customer inertia is when customers get comfortable with a brand and are loath to change it. It often takes a lot of effort to dislodge customers from an existing relationship, even if the current brand is doing very little for the customer. At times, when a customer is upset with the brand, if it reacts quickly and demonstrates genuine empathy, the customer often forgives the misstep. So powerful is customer inertia.

For a brand we used to manage, we once ran a sales promotion in which a select few winners of a lucky draw would get a car free. It was during the festival season of Diwali and hundreds of thousands of people purchased the brand to take part in the promotion. All entries received during the week were to be included for the weekly draw that would take place on the weekend and if unsuccessful, would remain in the reckoning for all the forthcoming draws till the end of the promotion.

A month into the promotion, the managing director of the company called me up. He was perturbed at receiving a mail from a customer who bitterly accused the company of not considering his name for the promotion despite him having purchased the product during the offer period, thus denying him the opportunity of winning the grand prize. The managing director politely asked my opinion on how the company should go about handling this matter of the irate customer.

Having assured the MD that I would handle it, I collected all the details of the customer. As a first step, I did a manual check in the system. Here I was happy to note that this customer was very much a part of the lucky draw. Since the main reason of the customer's angst had been proven wrong, I decided to speak to him directly. I called him up on the number provided and after apologizing for any inconvenience caused to him, heard out his grievances. His anger began dissipating even as he recounted his misgivings at being left out of the promotion. Having let him pour his heart out, I once again apologized and then went on to reassure him that his entry was indeed a part of our system and that he was very much in the running for the lucky draw.

He didn't say much after that, but a few days later, the managing director received a life-size card from the customer thanking him for the prompt redressal of his complaint and praising the brand and the valuable relationship they shared. The MD, without a word handed the card over to me. It remains an important lesson in understanding customer relationship management.

Chapter Summary

1. All entrepreneurs' one true wish is to serve all their customers' needs at all times.
2. To an entrepreneur a customer's sentiment is more valuable than the worth of the business, it's a reflection of the trust the customer places in the relationship.
3. Response to a query or requirement that happens after the customer need for support has passed, is of no value.
4. AI enables brands to be engaged with their customers, 24x7, 365 days a year.
5. AI brings responsiveness to customer engagement. This takes care of the urgency issues felt by the customer.
6. AI's predictiveness can actually eliminate issues before they arise.
7. Through personalization, AI can deliver unique solutions to a diverse set of customers.
8. Ninety-five percent of all customer interactions by 2025 is estimated to be through channels supported by AI.
9. AI-powered CDPs enable brands to carry out vast sets of valuable conversations simultaneously with the customer on a real-time basis.
10. A number of AI-enabled CRM and CDP tools can empower entrepreneurs to engage continuously and meaningfully with their customers.

CHAPTER 9

Overview

With an understanding of how AI can play a critical role in knowing, communicating and engaging with the customer gleaned from the earlier chapters, this chapter extends the ambit for brands by exploring how AI can enable a unique brand experience for the consumer.

- How AI enables brands differentiate between consumer needs and desires.
- How AI is rewriting the traditional laws of marketing.
- Why AI is the best friend of ideas.
- What makes AI the common factor among the best customer experiences globally.
- How to create a unique customer experience for your brand using AI.

Improving the Customer's Brand Experience Using AI

Starbucks isn't among the world's favorite brands without a good reason. The brand is always on the move, finding unique ways to provide a great experience for its customers. Starbucks uses AI and machine learning in their mobile app and rewards program, to better understand every consumer's choice. By understanding their customers' preferences, Starbucks is able to personalize servings and offerings, much to the delight of the customer. Then by suggesting accompaniments designed by Starbuck's Digital Flywheel Program, its specialist food and drink cloud-based AI engine, Starbucks is able to maintain the special bond that it shares with its diverse customer base spread across the world.

AI is the single greatest inflexion point in changing the dynamics of customer experience today. AI has enabled businesses in countless industries to understand their customers better and gain unique insights about their habits, behavior, motivations, needs, instincts and how they react to different messages. Armed with this knowledge and the omnipresence of digital channels, brands are now able to customize offerings to consumers and provide them with different solutions and occasions to interact with the brand.

Today, a food delivery app understands how different customers interact and engage with the platform. They can segment their customers according to hundreds of different parameters, least of which is heavy users, moderate users and occasional users. They have data that tells them: Which customers are experimenters or foodies looking to be the first to try out a new restaurant and its cuisine, which customers regularly write reviews of the restaurants they have eaten at, customers who tend to prefer one kind of food, customers who're deal seekers and those who are heavy weekend users and so on.

AI allows the platform and restaurants to provide personalized offers to each of these different categories of customers. Simultaneously this gives the customers the opportunity to scan multiple options at different points in time and enjoy a varied culinary experience.

Imagine a new restaurant has opened in the neighborhood. In the past, this restaurant would have to send out flyers and newspaper inserts, perhaps call in a celebrity or two, get some PR done and even after doing all that, it would take a while for the restaurant to gain positive word-of-mouth and draw in people with the regularity that the investment needs. In the past, the problem for restaurants has been that brand's visibility is restricted to its immediate neighborhood and it would take some time for positive word-of-mouth to generate sufficient walk-ins. A reason why location has been so critical to the popularity of restaurants. If your restaurant is in a good neighborhood, comprising of the kind of people you are targeting or if it is in a business block with a sizeable lunch audience, then such restaurants automatically attract a lot of walk-ins. However, rentals for such locations are usually high and they have to balance between pricing of meals and its impact on walk-ins in order to make a decent profit.

But thanks to AI and the revolution in food delivery and rating, a new restaurant can apply multiple strategies to ensure profitability. For example, if the cuisine is unique and new to the city, the restaurant can, on the platform, directly reach out to foodies or experimenters in the city, even those at a distance, because such consumers do not mind traveling a distance for a unique culinary experience. A restaurant can forgo a prime location and prefer to be tucked away in an alley and yet attract huge walk-ins, purely on the basis of its reputation on the app or website. Similarly, the food delivery platform, working in consonance with many tiny kitchens can offer a host of deals and offers for different customer segments: Families that prefer ordering on weekends, could get joint value deal from two to three different restaurants offering different cuisines that appeal to different members of the family. Compulsive snackers could be pleasantly surprised to find unique tempting snacking options pop up during snack time, each day. Customers favoring particular cuisines, could be the first to receive notification on the opening of a new restaurant serving their preferred cuisine and so on.

This is not fantasy; it is actually happening in many parts of the world. And it is happening across the board. Grocery shopping apps today have a good idea of the kind of products different household order on a daily/monthly/weekly basis. Based on order history, they can send reminders to customers to replenish products such as toothpastes, cleaning detergents, soaps, food items, staples and so on. The app or site could suggest options, hand out trials and provide interesting combinations that could appeal to different sets of audiences based on their purchase behavior and habits. Customers are only too happy to receive such assistance as it eliminates the worry of having to individually search for options and compare offers. The added advantage is that these interactions help the customers discover new vistas without any effort.

All of this together is rapidly changing our behavior. For the better. Today AI enables banks understand an individual's financial behavior and helps spot frauds, alerting banks to potential areas of theft. With an understanding of one's risk appetite, banks can provide customers with tailor-made investment solutions that fit their profiles. AI is not just making our experiences richer, it's also making them more secure, personalized and unique.

As the owner of a start-up, you must embrace these opportunities. These platforms are leveling the playing field for you. They're giving you the opportunity to run against and compete with the big guys. On equitable terms. Yes, they're big, but that would make them slower too. There are many layers for decision making and approval, not all of whom understand AI technology, the way you now do. Their decisions and processes take time to get implemented, because they have to factor in many markets, many stock keeping units (SKUs) and many logistical complexities.

You don't have any of those constraints. So, begin innovating. Most of the platforms you sell on or through, have people specially devoted to helping small businesses. They will provide you with credentials, training on how to use their systems and templates based on your needs. Use it. And then use your own ingenuity. Go back to them with a set of your suggestions. They may reject some and then accept others. Try them out. Keep the pipeline choked with ideas for your customers.

What is data telling you about your customers? What ideas is it igniting in your head? Build a variety of cases around these, bounce them off your team and their team, then implement it. That's the best way to know if it is working.

Remember the world has gone through a seismic shift this year. How is your brand adapting to the new consumer normal? How have those needs changed?

Being a start-up, your job may not be to recreate excitement for the category. Your task may simply be to convert people in your category to your brand. There could be minute differences between all the consumers in your product category. Understand those drivers. How many of them can you tackle innovatively? What are the modifications, adaptations you can make that can present a fresh alternative to your customer? What partnerships can you tap into and offer augmented benefits to the customer? Remember to use the A/B test when in doubt.

Customer experience is about kindling the romance in the relationship with your customer. It's about putting in effort to make the customer feel wanted and special. This is the essence of every strong relationship because you're not taking the other person in the relationship for granted. By providing them with unexpected moments of happiness and joy, you are demonstrating the extra effort you're taking in the relationship. Creating events and shared experiences that light up occasions, making the person feel cared for, emphasizing how much you value the relationship, a sentiment that percolates to the other. Such relationships are the ones that last long and remain strong.

Your customer is no different. The more effort you take, the more moments you create, the more experiences you provide, keeps the relationship alive. It brings sparkle to the relationship and ensures that the consumer always looks at you with fondness and affection, keeping competition away. Remember the adage, it is always cheaper and smarter to retain existing customers than to spend huge amounts to gain new customers, especially if you are steadily losing old ones. So, spend your time and money first in creating unique experiences for your existing customers that keeps the sparks in the relationship flying and your cash register continuously ringing.

No brand is too big or too small to create wonderful, exciting experiences for its customers. Nike is a great example. It continually breaks the boundaries of innovation to launch newer and better-quality products. It sponsors the biggest sporting events and partners with the biggest sports celebrities and stays true to its causes. Despite doing all this, Nike understands that while it may have ticked a lot of boxes for its customers covering things that the customers look for and value, it still needs to create special experience with them at the store to seal the deal.

Take the "design your own sneaker" experience at its stores. A customer at the Nike store can try out a Presto X sneaker bereft of design and graphic and then creates her or his own unique design signatures on the shoe. The technology used by Nike involves application of augmented reality combined with projection techniques. This increases consumer involvement with the purchase process tremendously. Consumers now have sneakers that are unique, like their own thumbprints, thanks to Nike and it's not a template or a random design. Once consumers have designed their graphics and reviewed it, all they need to do is take a food break and return to the store in a couple of hours and their own signature sneaker is ready.

Thousands of miles away in China, Alibaba's Hema store is doing the same thing with grocery. These stores have no cashiers, they're interactive and linked to the Alibaba app. Customers who walk in can simply scan the products and know how fresh they are, besides getting information about the other options available in the product. Once they're done, all they need to do is check out on the app itself.

The outlets have a live seafood section, since the Chinese prefer to personally inspect their seafood before they purchase it. In case customers live within a three-kilometer radius, their purchases are delivered home as well. These outlets have a unique robot restaurant too, where customers can scan the menu on their apps and choose their dishes, which will then be delivered at their tables by robots.

Similarly, Coca-Cola's decorative ribbon bottles and their "Share a Coke" campaign, stood out from the clutter because it provided a unique interactive experience for the customer, infusing the brand with an approachable and friendly personality, in tune with the times.

Customer experience is not the prerogative of big brands alone. In fact, it is a must for smaller ones, especially for start-ups. Like the headline of an iconic ad, if you're a start-up, you must try harder to win over your customers by providing them with better experiences. Designing better experiences should not fill up your mind with dread. Do not be intimidated by the negative sentiments of time pressure, cost, execution that jump forward and kill every instinct of creativity. Bear in mind that creating consumer experiences are not costs but investments you are making. The naysayers in all teams will be quick to point out that customers are not demanding experiences and are getting great value in the product itself.

But that is the same argument people give to all relationships. They ask, why fix, if it isn't broken? The problem with this defensive mindset is that it fails to take into account that once a relationship breaks, it's extremely difficult to regain the trust and faith from the customer. Even if you manage to pull them back, cracks remain and eventually the customer turns away. It's smarter to have a proactive approach to customer engagement and include a process that keeps your customers involved and committed to your brand. So, don't give in to those naysayers. Plunge headlong into brainstorming sessions with the excitement of creating a wonderful moment for those who matter most to you, your customers.

Begin by putting yourself in the customer's shoes and live out the experience of the customer with your category and brand. Often, things become more revealing when we set aside our professional biases and look at the customer simply as a human being. Just like ourselves. Find out what are the highlights in their lives? What are the tiny things they struggle with? What gives them little packets of happiness? Who are they close to? How do they travel? What gives them unbridled joy? What puts a smile on their lips? What brings a tear to their eyes? Who are their heroes, their role models, who do they worship, look up to? What are they proud of? What are they diffident about? What kind of music liberates them? What's a typical day in their lives? What features on their dinner tables? What rituals knit their families together? What values and messages move them?

There's so much to learn about your customers when you look at them, not through the lens of your brand, but away from the microscope. When you see them as real people and understand what makes them so special, you realize the extraordinary people they are and how privileged you and your brand are to be made a part of their lives. It's these moments that will inspire you to list out ideas that emanate straight from your heart and touch theirs. Many of these ideas may be unviable. Many would be ahead of their time. Park them aside, for they will come of use some other day. Sift through the gems you've listed out and amidst those wonderful ideas, would be a few that should be good to execute. The best ones have business objectives worked into them. But it's not that all good ideas have to be business oriented. Many may simply create goodwill. But as we understood from the first chapter, goodwill generates great value over time. Focus on building the relationship and in due course it will repay you with hefty dividends.

Let's assume, you and the team brainstormed and came up with a whole host of ideas about what you can do for your customer and from these, you have filtered out the three to four ideas that are exciting and executable. You now need to convert these ideas into executable packages.

For example, if you are a real-estate company that builds budget homes and you have thought up the idea of associating with an interior designing company to offer your customers design tips for their homes, a typical package would include detailing the following steps:

Who is eligible for the program? These could be customers who have made the down payment for the flat or customers who are currently still negotiating, or even customers actively looking out for budget homes.

How will they get the message? Since you should have the database of these customers, they could receive the message through a variety of media: text messages, e-mails, social media posts and even ads on realty portals.

Who is the interior design company you are partnering with? You need to have put in place the right partner for this program, ensuring they have the requisite talent skills and have done projects like yours in the past. Do try them out and make sure you are satisfied with their quality and service.

What is the benefit for the interior designing company? While the program may add value to your relationship, make sure that your partner is clear about the returns they are getting. In this case, for their ideas and efforts, they get access to your customers. Can you include their fee in the overall cost by striking a deal with the finance company? Because if the cost of design is amortized into equated monthly installments, the monthly outgo for the customer would become an affordable amount. That way the interior designing fee and execution is built into the monthly installments for the customers and the interior designing company gets paid for their services as well.

What is the benefit for the customer? While the affordable home would be a step-up for the customer, getting a professional to design it for them would elevate their lifestyle to the next level. By signing up, they get to see various options on how to optimize their space making the home look wonderful, all of it for free. In case they're keen, they can actually have their home furnished by professionals with the cost being built into their monthly installments, which increases only fractionally.

What is the benefit for the brand? To begin with, the brand is now successfully differentiated from the other realty companies. Next, by displaying an interest in the postpurchase phase of the customer, the brand is demonstrating its commitment to delivering a better life for the customer. By providing the interior design service, the brand is perhaps giving this set of customers, a real taste of what is design, lifestyle and quality living for the first time in their lives. By making the program affordable, the brand is empowering the customers with a tangible opportunity for upgraded living and not just on their wish list. Even for those who don't buy the program, this demonstrates the value the brand places in the relationship by going above and beyond expectations. Rest assured that this act will be remembered by them for a long time and the brand will be their preferred choice when they decide to upgrade or when they have to make recommendations to friends and families.

Who is responsible? This is an important aspect of the package because, it identifies who is taking responsibility for delivering the experience. If left to the interior design team or the finance company, the experience may turn out to be totally different from what was envisioned. The interior design company may believe this to be a place to try out their eclectic designs, which though extraordinary, could leave the simple customer, stumped. It may also prove to be expensive and not in tune with the cultural sensitivities of the audience. Similarly, the finance company may use the opportunity to sell more consumer durables and furniture to the customers that may be unsuitable with the design aesthetics of the home and may also inflate the installments, straining the finances of the customer. Remember they're your customers and you should not be handing them over to others merely because it is convenient for you. The thought and effort put behind creating the experience would be destroyed due to the lack of resolve to see it through. To make it worse, your customers would be the first to experience this. The initial excitement of the offer would quickly begin to dissipate as they find that they're left fending for themselves. Most would quietly exit the program and believe you to be insincere in your promises.

Therefore, the responsibility of the execution too, must rest solely with you. That way you will be filtering the ideas provided by the interior design team and also sensitizing the team to what your customers are actually seeking and what would be appreciated by them. Your team will need to set boundaries, manage expectations, provide crystal-clear briefs and ensure the output is relevant and usable. Similarly, thrash out the details with the finance company, make sure all packages on offer are vetted by your team. Be present or ensure that your team is always available during the customer's discussions with your partners, ensuring immediate course correction or clarifications happen. In this manner, your brand is not only providing great ideas to your customer but also taking responsibility for its smooth delivery.

How will it be measured? Every customer experience you design must be measurable. That way, you will know how the idea got executed, what aspects about it worked, where were the pitfalls and what could have been done better. Measurability also gives you an idea about how many customers responded, what were their key motivators, where did they drop off and what were the factors that induced conversions. No customer experience program is ever perfect, but when you measure it, you will know what to improve in it. A solutions-orientation will ensure that your program improves with every passing year, with improved understanding of your customers' preferences.

Use AI to create these unique customer experiences. The entire example I have given you earlier can be created using AI, which could help you reduce substantial time, cost and effort. Also since AI is self-learning, it will continuously improve and adapt to the situation. It will also provide you with data points and information about your customer behavior, interest and interactions with the experience.

The communication to be sent out can be automated based on the CDP you have in place. The entire experience could be conducted virtually without a single human interaction. The customer could take the tour and experience all the ideas and options that the interior design team creates on their phones through a virtual reality (VR) interface. Customers visiting the sales office, can be provided with an immersive 360-degree walk-through experience using VR headsets. This experience could be completely interactive, wherein, customers can use a dashboard or buttons on the screen to try out various options for the décor as they walk around in their future homes. A calculator on the side of the screen, could keep them posted in real time of the total cost associated with each option and in parallel also provide them with the equated monthly install-ment for each of them. As the customer walks around crafting options, they could start packaging each style and its associated cost with a unique label. These get stored in their cart and when they are done with the cre-ation, they have all their options ready to choose from. Now, all they need to do is simply provide the authorization and walk away happy in the knowledge that their dream home is taking shape. In case the customer needs to discuss the same with their family members, they could send a link of the shortlisted options for them to modify remotely.

All these design and décor ideas get saved in a library that become ready templates for other customers who simply prefer to choose from existing designs. The customer who has been a design leader can be rec-ognized on their social media platforms by the brand giving them a sense of achievement among their community and peers. The learning that the AI will get from such an interaction will be tremendous. You will get a repository of your customer segments that will be finely nuanced by their style and aesthetic sense. Their decision-making behavior, choices of décor and financial considerations will provide you with deep insights about the reasons for their choices. You can also measure the chatter their posts create among their community in social and other digital media and measure the kind of reach your program delivered.

This is just one case in point to explain how AI can help you deliver a superlative customer experience that can differentiate you from the rest of your competition. This is applicable to every category: Retail, fast-moving consumer goods, durables, automotive, fashion and apparel and even business-to-business brands. No one ever refuses a great experience. If you can think it up, AI can help you execute it.

Chapter Summary

1. AI is greatly impacting the entire customer experience process.
2. AI has enabled businesses in countless industries to understand their customers better and gain unique insights about their habits, behavior, motivations, needs, instincts and reactions to different messages.
3. AI can help brands segment their customers according to hundreds of different parameters and provide different strategies relevant to those profiles.
4. AI is currently being used by a number of industries across different sectors to create unique customer experiences.
5. Big brands such as Nike, Coca-Cola, Amazon and Alibaba have demonstrated how AI can help deliver a great customer experience that has a direct impact on their business.
6. Start-ups and entrepreneurs too can use the power of AI to great unique customer experiences.
7. A great customer experience begins with a brainstorming exercise to generate unique ideas.
8. Experiences should be designed keeping the customer in mind without allowing business bias to cloud the process.
9. Create packages out of the selected idea based on five simple parameters.
10. Use available AI tools to deliver and measure the experience programs.

CHAPTER 10

Overview

The previous chapters provide brands with a roadmap on creating brand value using AI. This chapter will enable brands evaluate whether they need to adopt AI in brand building.

- The need for enterprises to be judicious for resources.
- A structured approach to evaluation.
- The importance of timing in business success.
- The need for evaluation of AI.
- What is success and failure in business.
- How to evaluate the requirement for AI.
- The SWOT (Strength, Weakness, Opportunity, and Threat) analysis for AI.
- The importance of staying ahead of the technology curve.
- Criticality for having a backup plan.
- A model for evaluating AI.

The Balance Sheet

According to a 2019 study by Gartner, the biggest obstacles to implementing AI in organizations were: the perceived lack of skilled specialist, unavailability of the required quantity of data and an inability to measure results and understand the benefits of AI. Unfortunately, this has led to many companies and entrepreneurs believing that AI is a waste of resources. While it is possible that AI may not be beneficial for an organization at this very moment, yet the decision to implement AI or not, must be arrived at after following a rigorous and definitive evaluation process.

As entrepreneurs we are extremely conscious of every rupee or dollar we spend. Funds, whether internally generated or externally procured have to be disbursed judiciously. Every expenditure must stretch itself to do more for the organization. Every dollar or rupee that is available has many hungry avenues in an enterprise, all of which present a good case for use. While spending that dollar or rupee, an entrepreneur has to evaluate the pros and cons of each case and decide which avenues best deserve the money at that particular moment. It is not necessary that only the ones providing the best return get the funds; these are judgment calls that an entrepreneur takes, depending on which of these investments are in the best interest of the business from an overall perspective.

Therefore, an entrepreneur can choose to invest that money in human capital over capacity expansion, believing that investing in the human capital may better serve the objectives than a capacity expansion. Or the entrepreneur may earmark funds for a sales promotion over a new product innovation, believing that the need of the moment is to increase market share through an aggressive sales promotion, which may not be served by a product innovation.

From my decades of working with successful entrepreneurs and observing their decision making, what stands out is that, despite a well thought-through strategy, there is no guarantee that outcomes happen as per plan. Fifty percent of these calls turn out to be right while fifty percent fail. Often, the reasons for success or failure were outside the parameters considered. Sometimes, an idea might simply be too early for its time, or the market sentiment could be negative as a whole, at other times, an unexpected external factor may simply change the dynamics of the equation.

In the year 2001, seven years *before* Tesla, a brave and dynamic Indian entrepreneur Chetan Maini commercially launched his electric car, Reva in India. Unfortunately, India in the 2000s did not have the ecosystem to support start-ups, had limited customer awareness about the benefits of electric vehicles and lacked government resolve to support such a visionary idea. So, even though the Reva is a good product, it never got the kind of media coverage, funding and consumer attention that Tesla has had. Reva was perhaps in the wrong place at the wrong time.

Having said all this, decisions have to be taken. And it's almost always choosing one over the other. It's foolishness to try and distribute resources equally among all avenues. That way no opportunity gets what it requires and all will fail. Distributing resources equally but inadequately carries a hundred percent chance of failure, hence it is best to take a call based on one's judgment and put adequate resources behind those ideas with the best chance of achieving their goals. Sometimes the long term takes precedence over immediate gains. That's a brave call to take. Because long term doesn't usually come with a specific date. Long term could be anywhere from 3, 5, 7, 10 or more years. Will the business be around for that long? Would the parameters of today be relevant then? A long-term bet sounds good, provides a sense of belief, but needs to be evaluated as well. Long term isn't a solution or a guarantee in itself.

Hence entrepreneurs must be reasonable in taking their investment decisions. There needs to be clear and measurable outcomes within specific time frames. Once the call has been taken to back a particular avenue, then that process must be seen through right to its end even if it includes more investments down the line.

We once worked on a soap brand that promised a brighter skin complexion. Research and sales of related product categories indicated that a brighter complexion was a key consumer benefit and therefore our brand's proposition was both unique and unrivaled when it launched. Initially the brand's sales took off and this subcategory soon began attracting other competitors. However, in a few years, the subcategory's sales began flattening and one by one all the competitors died out, leaving our brand as the only major player in the subcategory. We tried a number of options to give the category a fillip—by launching product variants, bulk packs, facewashes and refreshing the brand's packaging regularly. We also attempted fresh avenues of communication appealing to different aspirations of the audience, regularly.

Despite all our efforts over many years, the brand continued to stagnate. At the same time, research continued to indicate that the brand's positioning as a complexion brightening soap remained strongly entrenched in the consumer's mind. This told us that while the brand had achieved its positioning objective, that position itself appealed to a limited audience among soap users. In short, women between the age group of 16 and 30, believed this soap to be the best complexion brightening soap, but did not find the positioning very relevant. One reason could have been a deeply entrenched fear that, in its attempt to provide a brighter complexion, the soap might be harmful to their skin.

The team then decided to expand the ambit of the soap's position. We worked on and tested an augmented benefit for the soap. This positioned the soap as delivering soft skin, in addition to skin brightening. By doing this we hoped to achieve two objectives: One was to directly offer a key category benefit claimed by the big soap brands and the other was to tackle the misconception that this brand had ingredients that could potentially harm the skin.

A multimedia campaign was launched and a number of activities were undertaken to ensure the new message got through to the trade and consumer. Eventually, although the message was well received by the consumer and the other stakeholders, the brand failed to grow any faster. It led to the realization that despite our best efforts, the consumer firmly believed that this particular brand had a powerful singular benefit of skin brightening and refused to accept any additions to this. Only those customers who desired this benefit were loyal to this brand and bought it regularly. Other customers didn't value this benefit nor accepted the augmented claims, preferring other brands in the category.

This clarified that we had indeed achieved a sharp, albeit narrow position for our brand and whatever we do, would not change this perception among consumers. The only option left would be to completely shift out of the current skin brightening position and attempt a repositioning exercise. The risk in this was to lose the existing loyal customers.

The team evaluated both, the negatives and positives. While its problem was that it was strongly associated with a singular benefit that no amount of effort could dilute, on the other hand, this benefit was important to a small but loyal set of consumers. After careful consideration, the team decided to retain the brand's current niche, as it was profitable and required minimal investments. Thus, the team over a period of time, through trial and error, resolved the brand's future optimally.

The decision to adopt AI practices to build your brand will require investment of time and resources too and hence must be evaluated along with every other option vying for the resources available to you. However big or small your organization may be and however limitless its access to resources, there will always be more avenues and limited funds. Taking a decision to include AI practices in brand building cannot and should not be taken up in a half-hearted fashion.

There's a difference between believing in AI and using a test case to build faith in the process. The first is like building a boat and voyaging out beyond the horizon, the second is like chucking bottles with messages into the ocean with the expectation that if there's a civilization beyond the horizon, they will hopefully read the message and showing more enterprise than the bottle chucker, seek this community out.

Route 1 may succeed or fail, but it will definitely change things. Let's take the worst case first. Even if it fails, it will ignite curiosity, drive the following generations to examine the voyage in detail; to understand why the mission failed, seek solutions to overcome the issues, build newer innovations to tackle those issues, send out more teams, continuously improvise on their engineering and sea-faring skills and eventually succeed. This will lead to cross-pollination of ideas, trade, increase of wealth and improved standards of living in the society fueling greater innovation, more effort and learning. In short, even failure will ignite evolution. If the first expedition succeeds, it would only crunch the timelines of evolution. In short, failing to achieve your objective is not actually failure! It's merely a learning process, a stepping stone in the path of success.

And what about the bottle chucking community? They probably won't exist for long. How many floating bottles do you know have stirred a global search? Not trying at all is what is failure.

Compare the two; both communities had the same resource at the start. One decided to build a boat and reach out. The other believed it was play-ing smart and safe. What do you think would happen to the latter? Soon, this community would stop chucking bottles, reasoning that it wasn't yield-ing any result. This lackadaisical attitude would soon permeate the commu-nity attitude toward exploration and stifle other initiatives as well. Before long, a time would come when they would stop innovating all together.

So, don't be the bottle chucker. Especially not with AI. Believe in it and start small. And keep at it, irrespective of progress or setbacks. This is an unretractable path for a good reason, soldier on and you will find your own path of success. As for the fence-sitters, my advice is don't waste time and effort in AI if you don't believe in it. Invest the funds in something else you believe in, to make it work.

If you have decided to step into the future, you need to evaluate your planned investments in AI for brand building, against all the other invest-ments you intend to make in brand-building activities, for that would be a like-to-like comparison. In case you are also evaluating the use of AI in other areas of your business evaluate each application of AI against their traditional models checking for the impact in the short- as well as long-term. It would be erroneous to evaluate AI in brand building against AI in manufacturing, for example.

It's from experience that I'm recommending this evaluation and investment in AI. It's strange but the very industry credited with building brands is the perfect case to cite for an industry that refused to adapt with changing times.

The advertising industry was once the most glamorous of industries. The steady decline of this mega brand creation machine into a listless and marginalized shadow of itself is the most fitting, albeit tragic, example of an industry that refused to invest in change and technology. The adver-tising industry was once considered unique, its heydays were in the late 1960s and lasted well unto the end of the previous century. There was no one particular reason that made the industry so alluring, rather it was a combination of many factors that lent to its enviable image.

To begin with, the advertising industry accepted and celebrated a diverse range of talent that included creative people who hobnobbed with thinkers and artists. Strategists who were deeply connected with sociologists, psychologists and behavioral scientists. Business managers who understood the intricacies of complex industries ranging from petroleum products to high technology solutions. Talent managers who knew which levers to push in order to get the best out of moody and self-indulgent celebrities. Technicians and craftspeople in varied fields ranging from photography, postproduction, reprography, printing, film making, editing, music, animation, graphic design, event management, transliteration and many more. In short, an ad agency was the single place a brand owner would go to in order to get expert advice and solutions for a wide range of deliverables that were mandatory for the creation and building of a brand.

Two other important aspects formed the core strength of the industry—the first was a close association and knowledge of the media fraternity and the second being their unique ability in creative communication development, its execution and implementation. The former was integral to devising the reach and visibility strategy for any brand as it provided agencies with knowledge about the performance of different media. In those early years, led by stalwarts, the industry exhibited vision, ability and planning to bring some order of measurability to various kinds of media vehicles, thereby expertly advising brands on where and how to invest their marketing budgets. Senior agency personnel also shared excellent personal rapports with their counterparts in media houses, enabling their clients to get special deals. This collaboration between clients, agencies and media houses led to the creation of many great entertainment spectacles including soap operas, late-night shows, mega sporting events and more.

The other important aspect was the assimilation of specialist skills that was critical to the execution of creative ideas that included: briefing, scripting and directing specialists such as photographers, artists, animators, film makers to get the desired output, then composing the raw material to create artworks, which are processed to make production material for publishing and printing. To deliver this, agencies often had scores of specialist talent on their rolls in each of these different fields.

An ad agency back then was a virtual factory with streamlined processes that ensured the delivery of creative with clockwork precision. This was the world that serials such as the infamous "Mad Men" series captured enchantingly, making it a unique slice of our popular culture.

The people who worked in ad agencies often carried a chip on their shoulders. Advertising folks were kind of misfits in other places and the unique culture of the industry, accommodated and celebrated their eccentricities allowing them to thrive and be their natural selves. With their edgy creative ability, exceptional powers of perceptional and natural outspokenness, advertising executives, soon became valued among the traditional corporate houses who formed their client base, to provide them with the "outsider's perspective" of their business. Soon, advertising executives prided themselves for their incisive and brutal honesty that was admired among clients and society alike.

The problem was that the industry soon began to believe in its own indispensability. By the mid-1990s a belief began to take root among industry personnel that their opinion was always right and began to develop a ring of an attitude around them. They had forgotten that it was the collective strength of every little part of the industry that made them unique, not their opinion alone. The industry leaders began hoarding the business profits and splurging it on themselves and among the most opinionated of their personnel instead of investing that money in developing and nurturing diverse talent, unique capabilities, skill sets attuned to the future, technology, knowledge centers, equitable pay scales, conducive culture and bringing in more accountability to brand expenditure.

And so, as it always happens, when you don't raise the bar, others will. In the early 1990s, software companies began providing specialized tools to help develop creatives. As prices fell and more software companies entered the market with cheaper options, it empowered anyone with average skills to design basic communication material for clients. This led to the rise of freelancers and motivated clients to build a small team of creative talent to do their basic creative work. This led to the control of the creative shifting away from the agency to the client. Next, as printing technologies improved, the role for intermediaries was greatly reduced and there was no longer a need for those massive number of technicians and postproduction experts in agencies. Soon printers directly connected with clients and agencies lost a big chunk of their business. Rather than collectively rise to meet the challenges of a shrinking business, agency teams began to squabble and blame each other. Then, in order to manage the egos of different department heads, agencies made the other big mistake—that of splintering themselves into smaller units of media, creative, design, events and public relations Suddenly there were too many specialist agencies with nobody among them to piece it all together for the client. The advertising agency was no longer the one-stop shop for brand building! As a result, clients began recruiting people to do it themselves. This led to the creation of large marketing teams who then opened the floodgates to the consulting firms to provide them with the "outsider's perspective." This was the final straw that reduced agencies from the position of being brand custodians to little more than suppliers of creative units.

The industry, however, continued to exist in denial, refusing to climb down from their self-perceived pedestals, even as photo-sharing sites and independent film makers directly began connecting with the clients. And then came the Internet, followed by Google and Facebook and everything changed forever.

In the new digital world, the old rules of measurability were thrown out of the window as new terms, customer behavior and social media influences took root. As business evaporated, traditional agencies began folding up or merging with younger digital agencies and the few large ones around have been reduced to creating campaigns for an increasingly irrelevant traditional media.

AI is a similar inflexion point. It's the evolution process that one has to adapt to. It not a question of should you but rather, how best to. Having said that, AI is not a plug and play system. AI needs investment in time and training. It's a culture shift that you are planning to undertake. Therefore, you need to fully understand the implications of going down the path.

There are some important factors you need to be aware of before you can wholly adopt AI. First, you must have sufficient data for the AI to train on and then apply to a task. In order to begin using AI, you must first be a data-rich marketing entity. If you don't have data, it makes no sense in beginning your AI journey. It's better that you stick to the traditional tools for the present but begin the process of moving to an AI-driven organization. This starts with the process of identifying, streamlining and collecting data from different sources and channels. Ensure that this data is correctly identified and labeled and is clean; remember if your data is corrupt, it will damage your AI journey for years ahead.

If, after your evaluation, you have concluded that your organization has sufficient data, you can begin the process of evaluating whether it makes business sense to shift to an AI-driven approach or to continue with the traditional method. To begin with, you must have a clear objective on where you are going to apply the AI, and to tackle which matter. This objective must be clearly identified and written down as a problem or opportunity statement. This is critical as it will provide the framework for you to apply both, the AI-based approach as well as the traditional approach and compare their results. For example, you may set your objective as increasing revenue, getting more referrals, improving customer experience, even smaller things like increasing customer engagement on social media platforms and so on. Choose your objectives wisely. Please ensure that the objectives are set for a significant milestone. Not a small meaningless activity of a few months and neither a complicated objective difficult to quantify in a finite period of time. Your objective should have significant implications on your business and must be a critical part of your brand-building objectives.

After you have identified the objective, use the SWOT framework to help you decide on going down the AI path or not. Here are some parameters to consider.

Strengths of AI:

Can analyze huge amounts of data instantly.

Can analyze complex data sets that are segmented by innumerable parameters.

Will provide various solution themes.

Will implement and self-correct.

Will carry out incredible amounts of tasks at lightning speeds.

Will achieve optimal efficiency.

Weakness of AI:

Requires lots of data.

Needs to be trained.

Requires clean data.

Cannot relate like humans.

Does not know the difference between "good" and "bad."

Takes time to learn.

Will make numerous mistakes in learning phase.

Can lead to embarrassing situations.

Opportunities for AI:

Availability of AI tools for different aspects of brand building.

The rise of computing power, cloud-based solutions and social media provide rich data.

Threats for AI:

Data privacy regulations that may impact availability of data.

Now based on the aforementioned information, evaluate AI and traditional methods for the objective that you have set for brand building. Start putting down all the resources you will need to achieve that objective using AI. This will include cost of the available AI tools, subscription best suited to your objectives, any cost you may incur in obtaining, cleaning and streamlining the data, time and resource required in training and testing the AI tool. Please don't be conservative, take bold decisions and account for the best. If you're going to do this exercise, ensure that you have left no stone unturned in accounting for it. Take into consideration inflation and cost increases. Factor in additional resources. Ensure that you have enough buffers in place. It's better to be safe than sorry. Because later when you implement your idea with enthusiasm, it should not happen that your conservative estimates work against you and cost overruns change the dynamics of your business.

I'm stressing on this based on important learning experiences in my entrepreneurial journey that I have endured. A few years ago, as the ecommerce industry was taking shape, I had conceived, designed, developed and nurtured a unique online shopping app for the traditional retail markets. This app called "Ezeeshop" was created to help shoppers at traditional marketplaces identify the right product for themselves.

The logic of the app was simple. Traditional shopping areas in cities had evolved to cover many square kilometers over decades and sometimes over centuries. Thousands of tiny shops mark every nook and cranny of these markets, each with their own unique and special wares, from clothes to home décor items to trinkets and accessories. The problem for the shopper always has been that they have a limited time to shop in these gigantic markets, unable to cover even a fraction of the area. So, when they leave, they feel dissatisfied, wondering if they missed a good deal. The app was aimed at quelling this sense of dissatisfaction.

On Ezeeshop, a shopper at the marketplace simply needed to type in their requirement and all the shops that hawk that ware could instantly connect with the customer by sending their products and price to the customer on the app. The customer could then shortlist the products and the shops based on their wares and locate them using the map on the app. In this manner the shoppers could cover the entire marketplace on the app, and visit only the relevant ones, thereby utilizing their time optimally and leave the marketplace satisfied that they had got what they wanted. The app would also feature ads from retailers and restaurants in the area who could target the shopper with offers, unique cuisines and deals.

The app would generate revenue through these ads as well as take a share in the profits of the product sold through the app. Over time, the information and data collected on the app would also provide large companies and retailers with invaluable insights on the shopping behavior of customers. These reports and information were to be another source of revenue for the enterprise. The concept had been tested in two to three marketplaces and the retailers had shown great enthusiasm for the app, displaying willingness to share revenue with every sale. The entire app had been built around this symbiotic relationship. However, after its creation, when we moved it to the beta testing phase, we realized that the fledgling e-commerce boom in the country had taken off with such a ferocity that now retailers were spoiled for choice. A few big ecommerce platforms that were funded by large venture capitalist firms, so dearly wanted retailer signups that they were willing to pay the retailer large amounts to participate on their platform!

This changed the game completely for Ezeeshop, because now the very retailers who were to be the primary source of revenue for the enterprise began demanding huge money to simply be listed on the app.

Having learnt from this experience, I always ensure that I have erred on the side of caution in the future and advice others to do the same.

Now that you have factored in all the requirements and resources for both options, begin a thorough and detailed costing of the same. You will need to account for time spent in training and bringing the program up to speed and also cost for the alternative you will use in the time that the program takes to learn and act independently. Ensure that your costing is consistent for a sufficiently long time frame that matches with your stated objectives.

Having done the costing for both routes in as detailed a manner as possible for the entire length of time that it takes you to achieve your objectives, visualize and put down the accuracy with which your objectives would be achieved. Here you can search online for case studies of companies that have carried out similar exercises or speak to professionals who have the experience of conducting such exercises. From these interactions, list out the extent of what was achieved in each case and thereby estimate what can be pragmatically achieved, over what period of time. This research will also provide insights of what additional resources, activities and costs were incurred as the projects evolve and the revenue achieved.

When you complete the collation of all data you will have three to four rows for both options—using AI and using the traditional method, as shown in the following table:

	With AI	**Traditional**
Expenditure		
Revenue		
Percentage of objective achieved		
Cost saving year-on-year		

When you have entered the figures for the two routes based on the calculations and your research, the answer should become clear to you.

What you might find is that the AI takes up a disproportionate number of time and effort initially, resulting in significantly higher expenditure at the start. However, as your process and system become more robust, it will require less time and monitoring. The system will also make a lot more errors initially, sometimes so basic that you may decide to throw in the towel in frustration. But as the process improves and the scale grows, the entire dynamics will change. The AI will become astronomically faster and self-improvising, driving the entire objectives several notches higher. The quality and level of interactions and solutions will be on a different planet altogether.

Chapter Summary

1. Entrepreneurs are perennially struggling with many avenues vying for limited resources.

2. The winning ones are those that best justify the utilization of the resource from a return on value perspective.

3. Despite the most in-depth analysis, there is no guarantee that investments will provide expected returns. At best one can expect a fifty percent success rate.

4. Timing is everything. Even the most brilliant of ideas may simply fail because they were too early.

5. AI is a disruptor and it has already disrupted the advertising industry.

6. The process of adopting AI should be well thought-through. Investments must be carried on through till a well-defined result is achieved.

7. AI is dependent on the availability of lots of quality data. AI has the ability to analyze multiple layers of complex data to build different solution themes. AI will also improvise and find the optimal solution to a task.

8. To evaluate the use of AI versus traditional methods, begin with outlining a clear objective that has a quantifiable and significant impact on the business and an adequate time frame.

9. Research well to detail out the comparison parameters for AI versus traditional method.

10. AI will involve huge cost and investment in the learning and correction phase of the project, but once it takes off it will be self-sustaining and a gamechanger for the business.

CHAPTER 11

Overview

This chapter explores the possibilities of what the future holds for brands and AI.

- AI's ability to replicating an individual's style online.
- Creation of the virtual you.
- Multitasking takes on a new meaning.
- Your consciousness lives on forever, online.
- The ability to bring characters and dead people alive online.
- The significance of brands speaking for themselves.
- The negative fallouts.
- The need for clarity and transparency in information gathering.
- Likely scenarios.
- The proliferation of data and leaps in technology.
- The advantages to humankind.
- How brands can benefit in this environment.
- The need to embrace change.

The Future Landscape

Microsoft has recently filed a patent for an AI chatbot that can learn from an individual's social media posts, emails, letters, voice samples and other communication material and then replicate the person's style of communication. In this way, AI can replicate communication styles and personalities of fictitious characters, historic figures and even deceased people. This could include friends, family, me and you. That's right. This machine learning algorithm will scan through all your social media activity, e-mails, letters you wrote in your teens, essays you wrote in school, speeches you gave, family moments that captured you, recordings of conversations stored in your devices and using all that information, it can in the near future, behave just like you, online. It can send out business e-mails if you're on holiday, post to your social media handles on your behalf, keep up regular conversations with those of your friends and family who you always wished that you could communicate more regularly with, respond to enquiries, send out reminders to associates and team members and even write your speech, represent you in webinars and virtual industry gatherings and perhaps deliver your podcast!

Now let's extend this conceptual thought forward to include more possibilities. The longer it lives with you, the better it will learn and the closer the likeness it will develop of you. Give that more time and soon, it will be indistinguishable from you. In short, it would have become your consciousness online. With one caveat—unlike you it won't be restrained by a physical body made up of cells that will age and die. Which means this artificial consciousness that has formed an identical likeness of you, will continue to live on endlessly and then eventually, will become you.

To speculate further, let's combine it with the rapid improvement in Deepfakes that we described in one of the earlier chapters. This virtual consciousness of you can merge with a virtual likeness of you and become you. Virtually! Now juxtapose this with our current situation when work-from-home is fast becoming an alternate reality. As we get more comfortable with virtual meetings and as the world begins connecting virtually, more people today are interacting with you digitally, than you in-person.

Imagine the amount of work that can be done with a virtual you by your side. Theoretically, virtual you can attend countless meetings simultaneously at every moment of everyday, 24x7! The concept of time zones will be meaningless because a virtual you sitting in California can at any time, conduct a meeting with a virtual me sitting in Mumbai and our virtual associates from Nigeria, Romania, Australia, China and Paraguay simultaneously, irrespective of time zones or language barriers because our virtual avatars would be multilingual!

Since these virtual representatives are immortal, they can carry on working on our behalf for an infinite period of time. In the gig economy, a skilled professional could theoretically be working on countless projects simultaneously at a fraction of the cost, delivering the same quality of work, provided the work meets the criteria for the application of AI.

So where does that leave you and me?

We have the opportunity then of improving our learnings, skills and knowledge and applying them creatively to develop unique ideas and innovations.

We will also have the time and the space to pursue the areas that interest us and the experiences we have been craving for, but have been unable to take out time for. Seems like a win–win situation, doesn't it?

The impact of such progress on brand-building efforts will also be incredible. Your brand will no longer be passive. It could now be an active, virtual personality with a visible presence. Your brand could engage in conversations—real conversations with all your customers virtually. Your brand can be always available, will represent itself in virtual brand events, award functions and perhaps one day even speak for itself! It could be treated as an entity deserving equal rights in your organization. It can have an equal say in deciding which celebrity represents it, on the creative quality of the ad, the media channels it would like to be present on and so on.

Superman, Batman, Spiderman, Mrs. Doubtfire, the Michelin Man, Ronald McDonald, Gattu, R. K. Laxman's Common Man, Goody, Mahatma Gandhi and every other character, cartoon, mascot and historical figure could now have a virtual representation. Initially they may have limited interactivity, essentially reading out speeches and messages of their earlier writing. But as the algorithm gets more inputs and learns from the wide array of literature surrounding these personalities, it could perhaps begin to create new messages based on the ideals and values these great legends stood for.

The world could always learn from Abraham Lincoln or Nelson Mandela, couldn't it? What would Superman have to tell us? What do you think would be his message to humans? He wouldn't be able to fly around physically, but he could inspire our youth, couldn't he?

What about brand mascots who would now have a life and a mind for themselves? For long their narratives have been controlled by brand custodians biased by ulterior motives of profit and business. But if mascots could have some control over their actions and what they stand for, will they continue to remain mute spectators? Or will they then start taking an active interest in the products they're representing? Will the mascot of an unhealthy snack or cigarette or soda continue to hawk it or will it learn from the ecosystem and begin to influence the decision makers in the organization to switch to healthier alternatives?

These questions and many other possibilities are what we may need to consider in the future as AI and machine learning gets more and more entrenched in our lives.

This brings us to the other possibilities of AI—the negative aspects. If an individual can be replicated in the virtual world, wouldn't it open the floodgates to cyber criminals, duplicating people virtually to carry out various acts of crime, terror and violence? If heroes and legends characters can be brought to life, can't the same thing happen with villains, criminals, bigots, fascists and negative characters? Isn't it possible that they too can be revived, brought alive virtually, to stroke hatred, bigotry and negativity that the world could do so much without? Just as there are technologists and companies adapting AI technology to bring good things to life, there also equally lies the possibilities of the negative elements in society, taking advantage of this progress to conduct their nefarious activities.

Therein lies the catch.

Indeed, a lot has been written about the negatives of AI and doomsayers predict a lot worse could happen. Indeed, some of the negativity and fear surrounding AI is not unfounded. But isn't this the case with all technological progress? When the steam engine was developed, one scientist warned that trains traveling above 60 miles per hour would cause asphyxia among its passengers. Another scientist scoffed at the idea of steam ships crossing the Atlantic as his calculations indicated that the ship would require to carry twice its weight in coal to complete the journey. The world has moved significantly forward from those questions and traversed countless other naysayers to bring us to where we are. While many questions are valid and deserve a course correction such as environment concerns, most other concerns often prove to be misplaced, giving us insights about how to approach AI and its applications.

AI, as I have repeatedly mentioned, is dependent on data. The question to ask is, where is all this data coming from? The answer is, from us. Whenever we're accepting cookies, ticking on "I agree," filling up online forms, adding to cart, uploading pictures, rating places, saving destinations on maps, taking surveys, clicking, sharing and commenting on social media and so on. Basically, any action we take today on digital platforms leaves behind a trail of data and information about our behavior. This is the data that feeds a lot of the AI engines. They greedily lap it up and use it to sort, classify or cluster us and then predict our behavior based on all the information we have provided. This information helps brands customize and personalize their products and solutions to match our requirements.

Currently, the argument against this approach gaining ground is that, when we agree to the conditions, most of the time we don't read the fine print and even if we do and agree to them using our information, we don't really understand or know how they're going to be used. In some cases, this is being argued as tantamount to a breach of an individual's privacy. There's merit in this argument as most of us agree, click and share things in all innocence, not knowing how this information would be put to use. Perhaps, as the argument goes on to explain, if we were to know in detail, the complete use and implication of sharing personal information, we would be more cautious and refuse a blanket permission to use all our data or infest our browsers with cookies, merely for reading an article, for example.

To credit those who seek greater transparency and tightening of information being shared, there have been cases to support this argument. Just recently, a senior executive I know was complaining of a strange incident that happened with him. He had called in the relationship manager assigned to him by his bank to understand some insurance products. While he had shown interest in one product, he hadn't signed any document and had requested for time to think over the proposed policy. Imagine his shock when the next morning he received a text message from his bank stating that his bank account had been debited by the amount due for the first premium!

Such instances are what raise concerns about the use of our data. We might in all innocence be agreeing to terms that tomorrow may be twisted to work against us. These well-founded fears are behind the drive to ensure equitable policies that respect an individual's rights while at the same time does not impede the progress of technology.

My sense is much like all the valid concerns about technology, this too shall be resolved to the betterment of all stakeholders. Perhaps in the future, we could, through Internet browsing dashboards control exactly how much information we want to provide a website with. If we wish to remain anonymous, that too shall be our prerogative. Of course, the flip side to anonymity would be that our need to search, find and fill will increase. The conveniences we are accustomed to will be withdrawn. Each time would be a first time for us. No more templates, no more prefilled forms, no more "people you may know," "jobs based on your profile," "favorite items," "recommended movies," and so on. Remember customizing information you wish to share for each site may also be possible, so while the tedium could be reduced considerably, it won't be removed altogether.

What's even better, is that perhaps based on your information-sharing behavior, you may in the future, be able to train an algorithm to share your information with other sites on a need-to-know basis. We could actually move to a world and an age where algorithms are conversing with each other figuring out what to share and what not to.

For brand owners and manager, this should not change things too much. Convenience is too strong a motivator for people to completely go anonymous. Indeed, there will always be a small number who prefer to do so—like those who, even today, willingly refuse to keep mobile phones or use the Internet directly. A similar set, albeit much larger, will be those who won't worry at all about privacy and continue to operate providing all their information freely. Don't believe me? Simply take a look at the crowds that continue to throng beaches, markets, pubs and eateries without masks in the midst of a raging pandemic. It tells you that there are enough and more who just don't care.

My guess is that the largest chunk will be the ones who will monitor the information they are sharing and are judicious about how much information they provide, to whom. Just like how people are realizing that being on all social media platforms doesn't really work and it's far better to be on only the ones that match their strengths, similarly people will begin to get more aware, choosy and conscious of the data they share on different sites.

Such a movement will prove to be beneficial for the use and adoption of AI. The information and knowledge that will spread as a result of these discussions will help create awareness about how AI works and its benefits. It will also help clear doubts and clarify all the misconceptions and fear that people have about the subject. Knowledge is the greatest accelerator for adoption of technology. These discussions will familiarize people with the process of sharing information and understanding its implications leading to more efficient use of AI, driving rapid adoption. Today, billions of people are yet to gain access to the Internet and the rise of AI-driven brands that make the lives of consumers more convenient, will only hasten easy and faster adoption of technology.

Meanwhile AI will continue to improve the quality of solutions in various industries. As the world evolves to cleaner and safer modes of transport, AI-enabled autonomous electric vehicles will soon become a reality. Home managers may find AI applications installed in their cooking devices, make cooking and other chores easier to accomplish. In the insurance sector, AI is enabling quick and early assessment of vehicle damage through image scanning leading to faster claim disbursements. AI applications in the hospitality sector aid in recognizing and understanding dietary restrictions of patrons, help in responding to client requests and automating bookings. AI will help us stay protected from phishing attacks and computer vision will help detect frauds in identity documents to great accuracy.

Weather predictions using AI have eased the worries of fishermen and farmers. Specially developed programs now guide farmers on growing crops that are expected to trend in the forthcoming season and help them find relevant audiences for their produce. Natural language processing will enable companies comb through the tons of accumulated data on their CSR (Corporate Social Responsibility) initiatives, bringing in accountability to the efforts and resources they have put in, over the years. AI can help doctors train on simulated surgeries and save time for them by providing minute details in super-resolution microscopy, as well to detect harmful bacteria such as *Escherichia coli*. In health care, AI algorithms can now identify and predict the COVID virus mutations, by tracking the evolutions that enable the coronavirus to evade our immune system. Today AI helps in the early detection of cancer, new drug development in the fight against Malaria and other mutating diseases and AI-enabled algorithms will improve molecule to participant testing, in the search to find a cure for obsessive compulsive disorder (OCD).

All of this gives us an idea about how AI is impacting every facet of our lives. It is spreading rapidly and finding deeper use in every aspect of our life. Unlike the popular notion spread by science fiction, it is not omnipresent, it's not general AI that will think and operate everything in the world as we know it. The AI that's being used is the narrow AI, focused on solving a particular aspect of a specific industry. There are some industries, which by their nature and evolution, have the ecosystem that is conducive for the deployment of AI. Marketing and brand building are fortunately one of them.

Here you have tons of data about customers, their activities, preferences, behavior choices, opinions, images, videos, selection, purchases and reactions. This data is priceless in enabling us to understand customers better, segment and target them with personalized products and solutions. Information also guides us in crafting the right messages, deciding who, when, where and how to target. Then on following up the conversations with experiences that delight them and processes that guide them through the purchase, use and finally enabling them to talk about their experiences with the brand.

This environment, proliferation of data and positive customer experiences have in turn attracted the best and brightest of talents to create and devise newer AI-enabled tools that improve the experience between the customer and the brand and build stronger relationships. Today, there are countless AI-powered tools that are attached to different aspects of brand building. Each tool is unique and has a specialty in tackling specific issues that marketers may face. These tools come bundled in attractive cost-effective packages for brands to adapt to their own unique requirements and use accordingly.

And what of the relevance of brand building, one may ask. Branding isn't a new phenomenon, different articles, thinkers and scholars have indicated that it has been around since the 15th or earlier centuries. Modern branding began in the late 19th century on the back of industrialization and mass production. Brand building is about unifying an identity, story and persona around a product, service or operation, packaging it in a manner so as to present the whole as larger than the sum of its parts. This has been applied to consumer goods and businesses recently, but it has been in use for centuries by kings, politicians and indeed the greatest branding example of it all—religion.

Religion is a great example of brand building and value creation, how an idea is packaged with its unique charter, personality, tenets, rituals and experiences. Every religion of the world has its own teachings, identity, rituals and beliefs that appeal to different audiences. Each provide people with direction, hope and guidelines on what is good and bad and how they need to conduct themselves. As a benefit, it provides an emotional anchor for troubled souls. It reassures people in a world where it's difficult to know good from bad, right from wrong, through its teachings, about how to be a good human being. This emotional bond that religion has with its followers is so strong and enticing that all the advancements in science cannot affect it. If anything, humans including many great scientists and thinkers are extremely comfortable with their religious identities even as they push the boundaries of scientific thought.

The power of branding lies in its ability to combine a set of rational and emotional benefits to an idea such that the net result has a combined value that is compounded many times over. This is a tried and tested formula that has never failed to deliver if done to a clearly defined plan.

AI on the other hand is a modern tool, an outcome of technology that is finding applications in the area of marketing. By using this tool brands can cut down complexity, gain insights, build models and deliver solutions that are personalized to their potential audiences.

Think about the opportunities that AI can provide different brands with. If your brand is in hair care, it can through a virtual interface, attend to countless consumers. On this interface, consumers could share images, videos and other data of their hair samples. Using this information, the AI could study details of each user, cluster them wherever relevant and understand the hair care needs of different users according to geography, race, gender and diet. Your brand can then mass customize hair care applications uniquely suited to the needs of each cluster and, if possible, to individuals at different price brackets. Imagine the kind of personalization this will deliver and the resultant trust that is built into the relationship.

As an educational institution, how do you adapt to this new world realities? How can you help potential students engage with your vast learning repository? How do you know what course is best for which student?

In the past, scores of competitive examinations were the only parameters for universities to judge the capabilities of students and offer them the course the student asked for. How intelligent is this process? Do students at that age really understand their interest and vocation? In many cases, the courses are chosen based on their market value and the potential for landing good jobs.

However, that is not the right criteria for choice of vocation. Students should ideally be advised by the university on the kind of courses they should take matched to their interest areas. If a university could chart out a career path for a student that illuminates the journey a student can take to achieve their potential, it would be life changing. AI can be the interface that studies the profiles of different students, conducts surveys among them to cluster and segment them according to behavior and taste. It could then customize career paths for the students, which outlines the options the future holds for them. Based on the interest shown by the students and through an iterative learning process, the AI could craft a personalized learning path that blends the student's natural instinct with learning outcomes, enabling the student to realize her or his potential to the fullest.

Together, Brand and AI form an irresistible combination that entrepreneurs can adopt to multiply the value of their enterprise.

Chapter Summary

1. AI is fast evolving. Soon it will be able to replicate a human being's communication ability.
2. Going forward, if this can be matched with Deepfakes that create a human being's visual likeness, it is possible to visualize a virtual avatar of the human becoming a reality.
3. AI would then be able to replicate brand icons, mascots, fictitious characters and famous dead personalities.
4. This opens up a world of possibilities for organizations as they can create direct interactions between their customers and brands.
5. The possibility of misuse of this technology also exists and use of AI will come under scrutiny in the near future.
6. Privacy and security concerns in the use of AI could lead to new laws and legislations being framed to regulate the capture and use of consumer information.
7. AI is making a huge difference in creating breakthroughs in various other industries ranging from health care, agriculture, autonomous vehicles, insurance and so on.
8. It is expected that AI will only emerge richer and better with governance and will continue to proliferate in the area of marketing by providing the function with better quality processes and tools.
9. Brand building is ubiquitous in creating value by compounding the rational and emotional benefits accrued to consumers. It is a successful philosophy that has wide applications and been highly effective when applied to a well thought-out plan.
10. Brand building using AI is the combination of an enduring philosophy with a game-changing tool that can help organizations maximize their enterprise value.

CHAPTER 12

Overview

For those whose interest in adopting AI practices has been stirred, this chapter presents the steps on how to start the process of using AI to create brand value.

- Understanding the basic criteria for adoption of AI.
- Developing the brand creative idea.
- The need for conducting a data audit.
- Criteria for creating the AI algorithm.
- When to use available tools.
- Barriers to adopting AI.
- Powering ahead.

Starting the Process

Luxury brands are loath to go online or use AI. They deeply believe that nothing can match the personalized experience and pampering that their brick-and-mortar store provide and are convinced that sales and conversions happen only in the controlled environment of their physical stores. Burberry was one brand that thought differently. An early adopter of AI, Burberry chose to adapt with the changing times and decided to provide the same quality of experience online, thereby mitigating the threat from e-commerce that was just taking shape, way back in 2006. Using radio-frequency identification (RFID) tags within stores, gave the brand an excellent insight on the shopping behavior of the consumers. This was compared with the consumers' online shopping behavior and this information was shared with the sales staff. Armed with a well-rounded view of the customer's needs, the salespeople could effectively serve their customers, helping them to augment their purchases with suitably matched items from the store. The brand also used data to identify and nix imitators of their wares increasing revenue tremendously. All of this led to an increase in consumer recurring revenue by 50 percent over the next 10 years. Besides this, it enabled the brand to take pole position in a world, where by 2025, 20 percent of all luxury sales is expected to happen online. As you can see from this case, it's never too early or late to start using AI.

To begin using AI for creating brand value, you need to have completed two steps:

The first is to have your brand workshop, discuss and develop your brand strategy and list out the brand objectives for the immediate term and long term. Based on this you should have developed a plan to achieve those objectives.

An important aspect of your brand plan is determining your brand's creative idea. The brand's creative idea is different from the brand's proposition. Let me explain. Brand proposition is an internal term that is used by the brand team to explain what makes the brand different and unique to the customer. For example, the proposition for Timex watches could have been, "Tough watches," similarly, the proposition for KFC could

STARTING THE PROCESS   163

have been, "Tastiest fried chicken," for 7Up it may have been, "Soda that's not a Cola," while the proposition for Duracell may have been, "Lasts much longer than other batteries."

A creative idea is expressing the brand's proposition in a memorable line or visual that connects with the consumer and sticks to their minds. The better ones are timeless and actually become a part of pop culture, like the creative idea for Timex, "Takes a licking but keeps on ticking," KFC's "Finger lickin' good," "The Uncola" for 7Up and the Duracell bunny, which by itself is a simple representation for a battery that keeps going on and on.

A good creative idea is one that instantly connects with you, it should bring a smile or an exclamation to one's lips. That's a simple sign that it is good. It should not be verbose or force-fitted. Keep in mind that a good creative idea may not necessarily fit your brief one hundred percent. Creative ideas cannot be bound by briefs, however well written they are. Remember a good brief is a lighthouse in the dark, it's meant to direct. It's not the end by itself. So, don't kill a great creative idea if there is some gap between it and the brief. The creative idea is the holy grail and great ones have a far better impact on consumers than any brief could have ever foretold. So, while evaluating brand creative ideas, use the brief as guide but follow your heart when you have to finally choose one.

The creative idea is the core around which all communication then gets built as per their execution requirements.

The second step is to have analyzed which of the areas in the brand plan is relevant for the use of AI and machine learning. This area should have fulfilled the two critical elements necessary for the successful implantation of AI:

1. The availability of large amounts of clean data.
2. Well-defined set of measurable objectives.

Bear in mind that developing your AI model will take time and therefore you should not implement it for any short-term objectives listed in your brand plan. Your AI needs to first prepare its model using training data and then begin applying that to the rest of your data. As explained earlier, be prepared for a lot of trial and error in this stage as your AI model will initially be off by huge margins. Do not get perturbed by the distance between the initial results and your stated objectives. Given time, patience and direction, the model will learn and will handsomely return your faith with interest. This understanding of the ability, application and use of AI is critical in ensuring your organization adopts this tool with the right set of objectives and expectations in mind, paving the way for a future where it becomes an integral and vital part of your brand and business strategy, proving you with the competitive leverage to maximize your business potential.

There are two ways to begin your journey using AI:

1. Create your own AI algorithm.
2. Apply an existing tool.

Both these routes have their own pluses and minuses, which shouldn't really be a concern area for you. What you need is to be clear about are the parameters important to you, to decide on going with either route. Going with either route has its own sets of implications; it is for you to decide on the one that most fits your need.

Creating Your Own AI Algorithm

This is best suited for large companies that have an established customer base, many employees, clear demarcation of functions that are further bifurcated and divided by different areas and specific requirements.

In such organizations there would already be tons of data available: of customers, behavior, purchase cycles, network, trade, past campaign metrics, media activity and spends, customer engagement activities, customer relationship management (CRM) programs, customer experience records, feedback systems, response mechanisms, research reports, brand tracking data, social media activity, large sets of followers, fans and responses, a history of brand activations, a measurement system and protocol in place, HR policies, ERP systems and an IT infrastructure.

In such an organization where the systems and processes are mature, there would be a well-oiled machinery to record and capture data. While it is possible that the data might not be updated with regularity and also may be scattered across various offices, all it would take is a systematic approach to capture it at one place, clean it and process it for use. Once the data backbone is in place and the system has been engineered to direct the flow of future information into the new system, the building blocks for creating the AI algorithm are in place.

The other key ingredient for creating your own AI system are people. You need to have data scientists and developers proficient in R, python and other languages used in AI. The number of people, skills they possess and the level of expertise will depend on the objectives to be achieved and the exact area that the AI model needs to be built around.

With people and data in place, you need to understand the plan from your newly formed team, set timelines and milestones and begin the process.

Please factor into the entire process, time and margin for errors and corrections. No AI system is going to get it right in the first few attempts. It will take time and regular interaction between cross-functional teams to iron out the anomalies and for the system to begin functioning accurately.

Applying an Existing Tool

This is ideal for mid-size to smaller companies that do not have the luxury of affording a large team of data scientists and programmers. It is also possible that in smaller companies the amount of data available is not sizeable enough to warrant putting together an AI system. Lack of data or too little data would mean that the machine will have limited access to learning from the training data; this would result in the machine learning limited things or wrong things that will snowball into incorrect classifications, clustering and predictions as the system begins applying this to the rest of the data.

Smaller companies do not operate at the scale and complexity of larger companies therefore developing an AI model, could be like taking a sledgehammer to fix a nail for a wall-hanging. Here, brand-building tasks could be simpler and manageable using off-the-shelf AI tools. Today Google, Amazon, Salesforce, Facebook, Mailchimp and a lot of other companies have AI integrated into their tools. I have also in the earlier chapters shone light on the AI-enabled tools one can apply for specific brand-building activities. So, all an entrepreneur needs to do is to search the right application for the operation being planned, explore the options in the tools suite and select the ones that are AI enabled. Using these tools may involve taking a paid subscription or making payment for different configurations, but these costs are not too high. The best part about using these tools is that they are user-friendly and need no coding or technical expertise. Almost all of them come with customer support and training modules on how to go about using these tools, all of which makes it extremely simple and easy for anyone to use and operate them.

Most of the tools provide dashboards and reports that help the user analyze the responses according to different parameters. The best part about these tools is that they can be implemented immediately and after the initial bit of time spent in getting comfortable with the formats and understanding the way to optimize the usage, they can prove to be really insightful and beneficial.

Implementing these tools in your organization's brand-building efforts will have multifold advantages. First, your organization will be more data-driven and accurate in its approach to brand building. This will have a ripple effect across your organization, which will evolve into an information-driven enterprise. The accuracy in the process will improve the brand-building efforts and the brand will be better connected, better informed and better serving to the customer's needs. Your teams will become highly charged and motivated because their skills are constantly being honed and their time is spent doing quality work. The use of modern AI technique will reduce the barriers to technology and clear misconceptions. Of course, all of this will lead to a healthier bottom line for the brand and the company.

The end result will be that, as your organization grows and becomes rich with data, you would have created the ideal groundwork to design and implement your own AI system suited to your unique requirements.

With this I come to the end of the theory on how to use AI to build your brand that will result in huge value for your enterprise. It still leaves you with the practical aspect of getting around to doing it. From experience I know once again that this part is the most difficult of it all. It's a bit like learning the theory on swimming but hesitating to take the plunge. Here's where the best of advice fails the test. Everyone nods their heads, says "I got that." But get back to the same routine they were comfortable with.

Getting started with anything is difficult and although I hope to have done a decent job in making it appear easy to practice, I know that a lot of you would still carry trepidations about the subject.

"It's AI! I'm not qualified honestly. What if I make a mess of it?"

Well, you won't.

I assure you.

Take my own example. I'm not a technician or a scientist. I am an engineer and I like to solve problems. Brand and marketing problems. I've always enjoyed solving problems for my clients by finding clutter-breaking ideas. This is what drew me in the first place to the wonderful world of advertising and communication and then as the problems grew larger and more complex, I grew into finding newer alternatives using a mix of communication, service and technology to solve those problems.

I still recall those instances of my personal evolution. Years ago, when I was working in the Middle East, the marketing director of one of the largest banks in the region opened up to us one day. He wished more customers of the bank would use the latest technology-based phone-banking services that the bank has installed at a huge cost, to pay their utility bills. This was a convenient option for customers as it enabled them to pay their bills from anywhere, at any time of the day. For the bank, it would eliminate the lengthy queues that formed outside the bank's branches, hindering smooth operations. It would also prevent daily altercations among people stuck in queues, in the binding heat of the region. However, despite its obvious benefit, consumers hadn't adopted it. Most customers hadn't understood how to operate it and the manner in which the bank personnel explained it, was technical and complicated for customers to understand.

It took me some time to figure out how the system worked and we converted it into a simple message of a three-step process. We captured this on a leaflet and distributed them to the customers standing in the queues, urging them to try it using their mobiles. The simplicity and convenience of this alternative caught on with the crowds, which quickly melted away on discovering this easy process. You see, people don't understand or care for technology. They understand convenience. If you provide them with a convenient option for something that is painful, using devices they are already comfortable operating, you've cracked the barrier of technology.

A few years later, one of my clients in the home décor sector wished to connect and sell their products directly to potential customers, in the city of Mumbai. The best way to do this was to constitute a home décor service that could be reached through a 24x7 call in number.

As an ad agency our responsibility ended with creating the communication for the service, but when the client requested me to execute the service as well, I took up the challenge. We created the entire process flow for the fledgling service. First, we put in a process of identifying, evaluating and appointing independent contractors who would be our partners in meeting customers and implementing our home décor solutions. Next, we evaluated and identified the right call center to manage customer enquiries and trained them to assign and coordinate inquiries with the different contractors. Then we trained another team to follow up with both, post the visit. Finally, we put in place, a monitoring mechanism that tracked all inquiries and analyzed the response at every step, assimilating the result into a weekly report.

An international client required that his website be integrated with all his dealers globally. There were a mindboggling number of products and variants that the client sold in different markets of the world. He needed this system to include a program that customized his range according to product categories available geographically, which the dealer could then download at the click of a button. Now this task again required a software engine to be developed. Not the job of your regular ad agency. However, the client believed that we had the right approach to problem solving and could put together people with the right skillsets to achieve the objective. Despite our limited exposure to programming, we approached the task by identifying the objectives, detailing the steps, stating the logic, defining the deliverables and identifying the right talent to do the actual development. The process went like clockwork and we delivered, much to the client's delight.

My experience with building AI tools too began with a similar desire to solve my customer's problems. My greatest regret in business has been to turn away small assignments from start-ups and entrepreneurs because they simply couldn't afford the fee. This desire to find a solution for them led me to develop BICO, Brief In Creative Out, the world's first AI-enabled online creative ad agency on which an entrepreneur could simply fill in a written brief and receive his creative in a matter of seconds.

My experience with BICO led me to explore available online tools as solutions for the new and varied needs of my clients, leading me to experience the field of AI, firsthand. These experiences made me realize how useful these tools are and how nonthreatening it actually is. My sense is, all the negatives we are hearing about AI are perhaps rooted in the fears of people who have never used it. Once I began using AI and exploring it to find solutions, I realized that this information must be shared with the professional world so that all brands and companies can benefit from its unique abilities.

So, my word of advice to you is, set aside your fears for they are baseless. Set aside your trepidations, for you will master this. Embrace this opportunity and grow with it, not only will your own stock and value increase, along with your brand's, but the sense of satisfaction and achievement you will feel at the mastery of the subject will be exhilarating and immense.

Brands are the face of organizations. Every organization is a brand irrespective of the fact that it may not have any product to sell directly to a customer. It could be a public limited company or a private limited company or a partnership. It is a brand, to the people who associate with it and who work at the establishment.

Now that you have a brand, why not make the most of it?

Putting a little bit of effort, following the process I have suggested will increase its emotional quotient and let people know about its unique benefits. These real and emotional benefits will multiply and compound and will increase your net enterprise value.

The rise of AI has made brand value creation easier for you. Sitting at your desk and using off-the-shelf tools you can get a better understanding of your customers, segment them correctly, message them uniquely and personalize your offering to them. This efficiency will improve your bottom line and exponentially increase your brand value.

Chapter Summary

1. The first step in using AI to create brand value is to develop a robust brand strategy that is broken down into a detailed plan for the short and long term.

2. The brand's creative idea is a critical component for the creation of a successful brand. Ensure it is unique and memorable.

3. The brand creative idea should not be restricted by the brief or business considerations. A good creative idea, even if off the brief will deliver better value than an uninspiring creative idea that meets all parameters of the brief.

4. The second step in using AI to create brand value is to identify the right areas in the brand plan for the application of AI.

5. The two criteria for identifying the application area are: The availability of large amounts of clean data and a well-defined set of measurable objectives.

6. Once the area has been defined, there are two ways to apply AI: Create your own AI algorithm or apply an existing tool.

7. Large organizations with tons of data, processes, ERP systems and the ability to hire specialize talent are suited to creating their own AI systems.

8. Start-ups with limited data and resources can ideally begin by using available tools.

9. Using AI is a gamechanger for organizations and will significantly impact the quality of work as well as the bottom line.

10. Fear of technology shouldn't inhibit the adoption of AI in brand building. By combining the power of both, organizations can unlock limitless value of their enterprises.

Bibliography

9 Applications of Artificial Intelligence in Digital Marketing that Will Revolutionize Your Business. blog.adext.com

1000+ Original Name Ideas Brand Name Generator. namify.com

Adams, R.D. January 21, 2021. "AI Space Farers And Cosmic Testbeds: Robust Robotic Systems Forge Path for Human Space Exploration." techrepublic.com

Adams. R.D. January 13, 2021. "Best robots at CES 2021: Humanoid hosts, AI pets, UV-C Disinfecting Bots, and More." techrepublic.com

AI Powered Consumer Insights: 3 Ways AI Is Changing CI Market Research. revuze.it

AIVA - The AI Composing Emotional Soundtrack Music. aiva.ai

Anand, S. January 09, 2021. "A Singapore-Based Coffee Bar Builds 'Ella': A Fully Autonomous Robot Barista Using Intel Technology." martechpost.com

Anand, S. October 18, 2020. "Google Introduces New Version of Google Analytics Powered by Machine Learning." marktechpost.com

Angela, C. July 26, 2018. "IBM's Watson Gave Unsafe Recommendations for Treating Cancer." theverge.com

Artificial Intelligence Marketing Solution. albert.ai

Artificial Intelligence MIT Technology Review. technologyreview.com

Artificial Intelligence: Examples of Ethical Dilemmas. en.unesco.org

Barker, S. March 30, 2020. "4 of the Best Predictive AI Tools to Improve Customer Experience." martechadvisor.com

Batesole, B. January, 2021. "Digital Marketing Foundations." *LinkedIn Learning.*

Benaich, N., and I. Hogarth. n.d. "State of AI." stateof.ai

Bhat, U. March 19, 2020. "Power of Artificial Intelligence-Based Consumer Insights." clootrack.com

Bhattacharya, J. August 17, 2018. "The Complete Guide to Brand Building." singlegrain.com

Blier, N. January 30, 2020. "Stories of AI Failure and How to Avoid Similar AI Fails." Lexalytics.com

Bradshaw, L. n.d. "Big Data and What it Means." uschamberfoundation.org

Branscombe, M. February 02, 2021. "Microsoft and the Workplace of the Future: How AI Can Help you Build More Productive Relationships with your Colleagues." techrepublic.com

Bulao, J. January 22, 2021. "How Much Data Is Created Every Day in 2020?" [You'll be shocked!] techjury.net

Burger, L. April 19, 2018. "P&G to Buy German Merck's Consumer Health Unit for $4.2 Billion." reuters.com

Burgess, M. November 18, 2020. "Telegram Still Hasn't Removed an AI Bot That's Abusing Women." wired.com

Burns, J. August 26, 2015. "Early Trains Were Thought to Make Women's Uteruses Fly Out." mentalfloss.com

CBS Interactive Inc. n.d. "Chatbot Trends: How Organizations are Leveraging AI Chatbots." techrepublic.com

Chen, Y. February 14, 2020. "7 AI Tools for Small Businesses Marketing." firstsitesolutions.com

Choueke, M. May 24, 2017. "Using AI to Gather Customer Insights." raconteur.net

Chuprina, R. January 8, 2020. "Artificial Intelligence for Customer Behaviour Analysis: A Practical Use Case." spd.group

Church, M. March 08, 2020. "Inside the NEW Amazon Go Cashierless Grocery Store." youtube.com

Clark, S. October 05, 2020. "4 Ways AI is Driving Better Customer Experience." cmswire.com

CNBC Reports. August 30, 2018. "Alibaba's Hema Grocery Stores are Changing Retail." youtube.com

Cohen, T., Chief Product Officer at LinkedIn. January 29, 2020. "Becoming an AI-First Product Leader." LinkedIn Learning.

Consumer and Market Intelligence Platform. netbasequid.com

Cotch, K. n.d. "Artificial Intelligence is Here: 5 Brands Using AI." toprankblog.com

CRM vs CDP Comparison: What's the Difference? pimcore.com

Daley, S. July 29, 2020. "32 Examples of AI in Healthcare that Will Make You Feel Better About the Future." builtin.com

David Beckham Launches the World's First Voice Petition to End Malaria. malariamustdie.com

De Rond, D. August 08, 2019. "Artificial Intelligence and Branding—How to Increase Brand value With Artificial Intelligence." thebrandberries.com

Deloitte Insights. January, 2019. "Cognitive Technologies: The Real Opportunities for Business." LinkedIn Learning.

Duckler, M. December 05, 2018. "3 Ways to Use Artificial Intelligence to Help Your Brand Grow." fullsurge.com

Elbermawy, M. n.d. "3 Ways to Use AI for Instant Brand Building." singlegrain.com

Fountaine, T., B. McCarthy, and T. Saleh. July/August, 2019. "Building the AI-Powered Organization." *Harvard Business Review,* hbr.org

Foushee, S.N., E. Little, N. Murphy, A. Saint Olive, and K. Shah. October 21, 2019. "The Next Wave of Consumer M&A: Searching for Growth." mckinsey.com

Franchisees. February 04, 2020. "Why More Hotels Are Owned." *JLL,* hotel-online.com

Fritschle, M.J. October 24, 2018. "AI Technologies Predictions That Will Dominate In 2019." aumcore.com

Gerety, R.M. December 18, 2020. "How New Technologies are Changing Farming: Robots, Remote Sensing, Machine Learning and AI." *MIT Technology Review,* technologyreview.com

Gillespie, C. n.d. "Giving up the Ghost: How Hinge Disrupted Online Dating with Data and Helped Users Find Love." mixpanel.com

Gohain, M.P. February 25, 2021. "AI helps track 56 JEE Candidates Who are Potential Impersonators." timesofindia.indiatimes.com

Goodson, S. May 27, 2012. "Why Brand Building Is Important." forbes.com

Guo, E., and K. Hao. December 21, 2020. "This Is The Stanford Vaccine Algorithm that Left Out Frontline Doctors." *MIT Technology Review,* technologyreview.com

Guttmann, A. January 17, 2019. "AI Use in marketing—Statistics & Facts." statista.com

Hall, J. August 21, 2019. "How Artificial Intelligence Is Transforming Digital Marketing." *Forbes Councils Member Forbes Agency Council Council Post,* forbes.com

Hall, M.D. September 03, 2018. "How to Get Quick Customer Insights from Analytics." smartinsights.com

Hao, K. August 20, 2020. "The UK Exam Debacle Reminds us that Algorithms Can't Fix Broken Systems." *MIT Technology Review,* technologyreview.com

Hao, K. February 17, 2020. "The Messy, Secretive Reality Behind Open AI's Bid To Save the World." *MIT Technology Review.* technologyreview.com

Hao, K. January 08, 2021. "Five Ways to Make AI a Greater Force for Good in 2021." *MIT Technology Review,* technologyreview.com

Hao, K. January 22, 2021. "AI Could Make Healthcare Fairer—By Helping Us Believe What Patients Say." *MIT Technology Review,* technologyreview.com

Harwell, D. November 06, 2019. "Hirevue's AI Face-Scanning Algorithm Increasingly Decides Whether You Deserve the Job." thewashingtonpost.com

Heaven, W. June 04, 2020. "This Startup is using AI to Give Workers a "Productivity Score."" *MIT Technology Review.* technologyreview.com

Heaven, W.D. October 15, 2020. "Artificial General Intelligence: Are We Close, And Does It Even Make Sense to Try?" *MIT Technology Review,* technologyreview.com

Henderson, B. n.d. "5 A.I. Tools Your Company Can Use Right Now." inc.com

Horie, N., Associate Director of Technology Strategy at edit.co.uk. January 22, 2020. "How the Influence of Google on AI is Becoming Key to Business Success." information-age.com

Hughes, B. August 17, 2019. "6 AI Business Tools for Entrepreneurs on a Budget." entrepreneur.com

Hughes, O. January 05, 2021. "Microsoft Wants to use AI to Turn Your Friends and Family into 3D Chatbots." techrepublic.com

Illa, D. April 15, 2019. "Gathering insights in Google Analytics can be as Easy as A-B-C by Growth Marketing." Google Analytics.

Imanuel. n.d. "Top 12 Customer Intelligence Platforms in 2020—Reviews, Features, Pricing, Comparison—PAT RESEARCH: B2B Reviews, Buying Guides & Best Practices." predictiveanalyticstoday.com

Insights in Association with Genesys. April 28, 2020. "How AI is Changing The Customer Experience." *MIT Technology Review*, technologyreview.com

Johnson, E. April 29, 2020. "How Companies Use AI to Improve Brand Management." jeffbullas.com

Johnson, E., Expert Commentator. March 31, 2020. "How Brand Management can be Enhanced in the Age of AI." smartinsights.com

Kay, D. February, 2020. "Customer Service Using AI and Machine Learning." LinkedIn Learning.

Kearsey, R. n.d. "How AI Is Taking Brand Marketing to the Next Level." adlibweb.com

Knight, W. October 09, 2020. "Sales Calls Have Gone Virtual, and AI Is Listening In." wired.com

Kopanakis, J. n.d. "How Artificial Intelligence Will Enhance Brand Management." mentionlytics.com

Kovalenko, O. June 23, 2020. "5 Most Valuable Applications of Machine Learning in Retail." spd.group

Krishnan, P.R. n.d. "Machine-First Delivery Model: AI Implementation in Business." tcs.com

Kundariya, H. August 12, 2020. "Is AI Going to Disrupt the Marketing Industry?" readwrite.com

Larson, K., and J. Klein. July 2016. "Google BrandLab: The Best Tools for Consumer Insights." thinkwithgoogle.com

Lim, S. 2020. "3 Types of Customer Insights that A.I. Will Change." remesh.ai

Lister, M. August 26, 2019. "33 Mind-Boggling Instagram Stats & Facts." wordstream.com

Magana, G. July 06, 2018. "Alibaba is Piloting Fashion AI Technology." businessinsider.com

Marr, B. September 25, 2017. "The Amazing Ways Burberry Is Using Artificial Intelligence And Big Data To Drive Success." forbes.com

Marr, B., Contributor. December 09, 2019. "The 10 Best Examples of How Companies Use Artificial Intelligence in Practice." forbes.com

Marvin, R. November 12, 2018. "10 Steps to Adopting Artificial Intelligence in Your Business." in.pcmag.com

McDonald, M. November, 2019. "AI in Business Essential Training." LinkedIn Learning

McGoldrick, J. Febuary 26, 2020. "AI Is Changing How Brands Develop Creative - Here's What the Future Is Looking Like." martechseries.com

Mendoza, N.F. February 11, 2020. "5 key AI trends in Customer Engagement." techrepublic.com

Moreno, L. August 28, 2019. "10 Impressive Examples of AI in Marketing." blog.socialmediastrategiessummit.com

Morse, B. April 20, 2017. "Become Part of the Story with the Marvel Comics Chatbot." marvel.com

MIT Technology Review Insights in Association with Arm MIT Technology Review. November 30, 2020. "A New Horizon: Expanding the AI Landscape." technologyreview.com

Njamfa, O. May 24, 2019. "5 ways AI can Transform Customer Insight for Your Business." customerthink.com

Odden, L. n.d. "AI in Marketing: 54 Artificial Intelligence (AI) Marketing Tools." toprankblog.com

Offsey S. n.d. "What is Customer Journey Analytics?" pointillist.com

Ohashi, A. February, 2019. "Learning XAI: Explainable Artificial Intelligence." LinkedIn Learning.

Ovsiienko, M. June 18, 2019. "5 Success Stories of AI in E-commerce." neoteric.eu

Patel, N. n.d. "How to Use Google Analytics to Shape Your Marketing Strategy." neilpatel.com

Patil, A., and J.E. Bromwich. September 29, 2020. "How It Feels When Software Watches You Take Tests." nytimes.com

Polonski, V. May 25, 2018. "Why AI Can't Solve Everything." theconversation.com

Porwal, H. September 20, 2016. "10 A.I. Tools to Help Your Business." *Tool Owl*. venturebeat.com

Poulson, B. January, 2019. "AI Accountability Essential Training." LinkedIn Learning.

Power, B. May 30, 2017. "How Harley-Davidson Used Artificial Intelligence to Increase New York Sales Leads by 2,930%." *Harvard Business Review*, hbr.org

Prater, J.D. July 30, 2017. "Improve Customer Insights with these 5 Google Analytics Integrations." *Marketing and Growth Hacking.* blog.markgrowth.com

Preetipadma. June 01, 2020. "How is AI Empowering the Weather Forecasting Technology?" analyticsinsight.net

Product Launch in D2C Era (2021 Guide). revuze.it

Raab, D. October 05, 2020. "What's a Customer Data Platform? The Ultimate Guide to CDPs." blog.hubspot.com

Razzaq, A. January 18, 2021. "Google AI Introduces ToTTo: A Controlled Table-to-Text Generation Dataset Using Novel Annotation Process." marktechpost.com

Regalado, A. December 31, 2020. "Worst Technology Failures of 2020." *MIT Technology Review*, technologyreview.com

Rora, C., Expert Commentator. January 13, 2020. "How AI is Transforming the Future of Digital Marketing." smartinsights.com

Rose, D. April, 2018. "Artificial Intelligence Foundations: Neural Networks." LinkedIn Learning.

Rose, D. March, 2018. "Artificial Intelligence Foundations: Machine Learning." LinkedIn Learning.

Rose, D. November, 2017. "Artificial Intelligence Foundations: Thinking Machines." LinkedIn Learning.

Ruma, L., and S. Jockusch. October 28, 2020. "With Trust in AI, Manufacturers Can Build Better." *MIT Technology Review*, In association with Siemens Digital Industries Software. technologyreview.com

Schneider, J., and J. Hall. April 2011. "Why Most Product Launches Fail." *Harvard Business Review.*

Scott, G. n.d. "Why Brand Building Is Important by" forbes.com

Sehgal, S. February, 2020. "Artificial Intelligence for Cybersecurity." LinkedIn Learning.

Self - Text Analytics Tool For eCommerce Opinions. revuze.it

Sharma, A. May 03, 2019. "4 Big Brands That Use AI & ML to Improve Customer Experience." signitysolutions.com

Shenwai, T. January 06, 2021. "Open AI Introduces DALL·E: A Neural Network That Creates Images from Text Descriptions." marktechpost.com

Shenwai, T. January 11, 2021. "Introducing 'Chitrakar' A New AI System That Converts Images of a Human Face into the Jordan Curve." martechpost.com

Shroff, R. July 24, 2020. "Preparing Corporations for Artificial Intelligence Adoption." towardsdatascience.com

Shukla, S. December 03, 2019. "Using AI to Better Understand and Engage Your Customers." *Microsoft Dynamics 365 Blog*, cloudblogs.microsoft.com

Simone, S. December 22, 2020. "AI Predictions for 2021." dbta.com

Simonite, T. February 01, 2018. "What Defines Artificial Intelligence? The Complete WIRED Guide." wired.com

Simonite, T. October 02, 2020. "AI Can Help Patients—but Only If Doctors Understand It." wired.com

Singh, A.N. May 03, 2019. "8 ways to Gain Consumer Insights Using AI." medium.com

Skai. February 25, 2019. "How Many Google Searches Per Day Are There?" skai.io

Sloan, W. August 21, 2012. "The Reva Electric Car Story - In Conversation with the Creator, Chetan Maini." yourstory.com

Smith, K. June 01, 2019. "53 Incredible Facebook Statistics and Facts." brandwatch.com

Soegaard, M. n.d. "Occam's Razor: The Simplest Solution is Always the Best." *Interaction Design Foundation (IxDF).* interaction-design.org

Soni, Y. January 06, 2020. "How Digital Marketers Are Leveraging AI Tools and Automation in Advertising." Inc42.com

Souza, D. December 18, 2020. "The Kitchen of the Future is Here, It's Just Not Evenly Distributed." *MIT Technology Review.* technologyreview.com

Stanford Encyclopaedia of Philosophy. April 30, 2020. "Ethics of Artificial Intelligence and Robotics." plato.stanford.edu

Steinmann, L. October 23, 2019. "How to use AI for Small Business." microsoft.com

Sterne, J., and Madecraft. November, 2020. "Artificial Intelligence for Marketing." LinkedIn Learning.

Stokes. R. n.d. "5 Ways Artificial Intelligence Can Help Your Brand Grow." convinceandconvert.com

Strong, J., and Team MIT Technology Review. October 14, 2020. "AI Reads Human Emotions. Should It?" *MIT Technology Review.* technology review.com

Suresh, P. July 21, 2020. "Most Valuable Brands of 2020: At $415 Billion, The Top Company Beats Apple, Google and Microsoft." cnbctv18.com

Sychyk, A. March 13, 2020. "Does Your Business Really Need an AI Solution?" readwrite.com

The Future of Work. roberthalf.com

The United States of Artificial Intelligence. cbinsights.com, March 17, 2021.

Thiel, W. n.d. "The Role of AI in Customer Experience." pointillist.com

Think Future of Marketing. thinkwithgoogle.com

Tran, K. July 12, 2018. "Google is capitalizing on AI in Marketing." businessinsider.com

Verma, S. April 20, 2019. "Explained: The Rise and Fall of Private Airlines." indianexpress.com

Vigliarolo, B. January 25, 2021. "Gartner: The future of AI is not as Rosy as Some Might Think." techrepublic.com

VOA News. August 10, 2020. "Chatbots and Telemedicine Join Vietnam's COVID-19 Fight." voanews.com

Vuleta, B. January 28, 2021. "How Much Data Is Created Every Day?" seedscientific.com

Walch, K. December 29, 2019. "Ethical Concerns of AI." forbes.com

Web Analytics and Consumer Insights Schleicher Marketing. schleicher marketing.com

What Are the Ethical Problems in Artificial Intelligence? geeksforgeeks.org, June 02, 2020

What is a Customer Data Platform? How is it Different from a DMP or CRM? econsultancy.com

Why Customer Analytics Are the Key to Creating Value. February 2016. thinkwithgoogle.com

WIRED Brand Lab for H2O.ai. "The push for responsible AI." wired.com

About the Author

Rajan Narayan holds a degree in Electrical and Electronics engineering from the prestigious Manipal Institute of Technology—one of India's designated Institutes of Eminence and subsequently did his MBA from Mumbai University. With over 25 years of experience in the field of marketing communications, Rajan has worked in some of the world's best communication groups, rising up their ranks rapidly. He has helped build brands across diverse categories, in India and globally. A certified Master's in Digital Marketing, Rajan has provided strategic advice to start-ups on digital transformation, distribution strategies, new product launches, entering new markets, rural marketing, consumer research, media planning, web, digital and social media marketing. In short, a career defined by helping entrepreneurs identify their opportunities or deep-rooted problems and then creating holistic solutions for them, ensuring their business growth. Rajan ran a full-service, network advertising agency independently and successfully for NINE years as President and CEO, building a roster of blue-chip clients and delivering high growth and profits consistently. He then founded his own marketing consulting firm, Lonely Cloud Consulting in 2015, and has been successful in providing brand and marketing advise to entrepreneurs both in India and globally, helping them multiply the value of their enterprise rapidly. He believes that entrepreneurs are critical to the growth of the economy and they need the power of branding to help differentiate themselves among consumers to create enormous value. Given their resource constraints, technology is an important conduit through which entrepreneurs and start-ups can level the playing field against large companies and build powerful and valuable brands. This led Rajan to create BICO: Brief In, Creative Out, the world's first artificial intelligence (AI)-enabled online creative ad agency. Rajan has enabled entrepreneurs realize over USD 2 billion in terms of brand value. His mission is to help more of them unlock the full potential of their enterprise value using a combination of brand strategy and AI technology.

He can be reached at rajan.narayan@thelonelycloudconsulting.com
LinkedIn: https://linkedin.com/in/rajanlnarayan/

Index

OTHER TITLES IN THE MARKETING COLLECTION

Naresh Malhotra, Georgia Tech, Editor

- *Branding & AI* by Chahat Aggarwal
- *Stand Out!* by Brian McGurk
- *The Coming Age of Robots* by George Pettinico and George R. Milne
- *Market Entropy* by Rajagopal
- *Decoding Customer Value at the Bottom of the Pyramid* by Ritu Srivastava
- *Qualitative Marketing Research* by Rajagopal
- *Social Media Marketing* by Alan Charlesworth
- *Employee Ambassadorship* by Michael W Lowenstein
- *Critical Thinking for Marketers, Volume I* by David Dwight, David Soorholtz, and Terry Grapentine
- *Critical Thinking for Marketers, Volume II* by David Dwight, David Soorholtz, and Terry Grapentine
- *Relationship Marketing Re-Imagined* by Naresh Malhotra, Can Uslay, and Ahmet Bayraktar
- *Marketing Plan Templates for Enhancing Profits* by Elizabeth Rush Kruger
- *Launching New Products* by John C. Westman and Paul Sowyrda
- *Market Sensing Today* by Melvin Prince and Constantinos-Vasilios Priporas

Concise and Applied Business Books

The Collection listed above is one of 30 business subject collections that Business Expert Press has grown to make BEP a premiere publisher of print and digital books. Our concise and applied books are for...

- Professionals and Practitioners
- Faculty who adopt our books for courses
- Librarians who know that BEP's Digital Libraries are a unique way to offer students ebooks to download, not restricted with any digital rights management
- Executive Training Course Leaders
- Business Seminar Organizers

Business Expert Press books are for anyone who needs to dig deeper on business ideas, goals, and solutions to everyday problems. Whether one print book, one ebook, or buying a digital library of 110 ebooks, we remain the affordable and smart way to be business smart. For more information, please visit www.businessexpertpress.com, or contact sales@businessexpertpress.com.

www.ingramcontent.com/pod-product-compliance
Lightning Source LLC
Chambersburg PA
CBHW061305220326
41599CB00026B/4743